Household Hints

Hints

NATURALLY

Publisher and Creative Director: Nick Wells
Senior Project Editor: Catherine Taylor
Picture Research: Catherine Taylor, Charlotte McLean and Katie Pimlott
Contributing Photographer: Paul Forrester
Art Director: Mike Spender
Digital Design and Production: Chris Herbert

FLAME TREE PUBLISHING
6 Melbray Mews, Fulham
London SW6 3NS
United Kingdom

www.flametreepublishing.com

First published in 2019

19 21 23 22 20
1 3 5 7 9 10 8 6 4 2

© 2019 Flame Tree Publishing

Diane and Jon Sutherland are professional writers. They have written a wide variety of titles, spanning household hints, travel, children's, military history and education. They have won several literary prizes, including New York Libraries' Best of Reference and Booklist Editors' Choice Award.

Maria Costantino has written such titles as *The Handbook: Household Hints & Tips, DIY Encyclopedia, First Aid Pocket Guide* and many other books on food, drink, art, design and fashion. She teaches Historical, Critical and Theoretical Studies at several universities in England.

Liz Keevill and Kevin Eyres are professional writers and journalists. Liz spent many years as a consumer journalist on *Good Housekeeping* and *Ideal Home* magazines and has written books on interior design, furnishings, and general housekeeping matters. Kevin writes on travel, the arts and interior lighting design as well as being a commercial copywriter. They are both interested in anything that reduces the toxic content of everyday things.

A CIP Record for this book is available from the British Library upon request.

ISBN 978-1-78755-765-9

Printed in China

Picture credits: © Flame Tree Publishing Ltd: 11 & 104bl, 23, 42b, 68b, 69, 70, 89t, 99, 232bl, 233, 241t, 243bl, 243tl, 243r, 247l, 250t. All other images are courtesy of **Shutterstock.com** and © the following contributors: 1 Viktar Malyshchyts; 3 Jonathan Vasata; 5bl Scott L. Williams; 5br rebvt; 5tl, 8, 83br, 182, 198 matka_Wariatka; 5tr Aleksej Starostin; 6 Andre Klaassen; 7bl Ed Isaacs; 7t Picsfive; 9 Igor Smichkov; 10 StockLite; 12 ODM; 13, 75 Igor Dutina; 14 Magdalena Bujak; 15 Color; 16 Natalia D.; 17b Alistair Cotton; 17t fredredhat; 18, 109 Dmitry Naumov; 19, 171 Sandra Cunningham; 20 & 52 Lepas; 21 Darren A Hubley; 22b Yurchyks; 22tl Nessi; 24b 5AM Images; 24t aceshot1; 25 Konovalikov Andrey; 26b Margo Harrison; 26t terekhov igor; 27 Katerina Havelkova; 28 Grauvision; 29, 84 Peter Gudella; 30, 91 Stephen VanHorn; 31 Lori Sparkia; 32 Terry Underwood Evans; 33 Freddy Eliasson; 34 Olga Chernetskaya; 35 Baloncici; 36 khz; 37 PAUL ATKINSON; 38 Matt Ragen; 39 Germany Feng; 40 Lisa Turay; 41 Mats; 42t Romanchuk Dimitry; 43 microstocker; 44 photogl; 46 & 67b Tiplyashin Anatoly; 47 Hallgerd; 48 Photoroller; 49, 166 Julija Sapic; 50 Tom Baker; 51b cosma; 51 M.E. Mulder; 53t Daniel Krylov; 54, 165, 189 Elena Elisseeva; 55 Ragne Kabanova; 56b Anne Kitzman; 56t SeDmi; 57 trailexplorers; 58 Tomasz Trojanowski; 59 Irina Fischer; 60, 231b Paul Cowan; 61 Pavelk; 62 Muriel Lasure; 63 Jon Kasawa; 64 Brian A Jackson; 65, 117, 225, 240 Monkey Business Images; 66 Alistair Scott; 67t Daniel Goodings; 68t Jeffrey Van Daele; 71, 82t, 167 Diego Cervo; 72 & 83t Dan Thomas Brostrom; 73 Eric Gevaert; 74 Jennifer Nickert; 76 Paul Krugloff; 77 Picsfive; 78 Petro Feketa; 79 Agb; 80 Babusi Octavian Florentin; 81 Martin Smith; 82b ostill; 85b Africa Studios; 85t Ivaschenko Roman; 86 David W. Leindecker; 87 Anthony Harris; 88 Carly Rose Hennigan; 89b Vladimir Melnik; 90 pixelman; 93, 230b Mike Flippo; 94 Ramona Heim; 95, 139 Joy Brown; 96 & 168 Pefkos; 97 sharon kingston; 98 Kameel4u; 100 Jiri; 101 Patrick McCall; 102 Vasily Mulyukin; 103 kreego; 104t Nancy Kennedy; 105 Kimmit; 106 Cherick; 107 Kathy Piper; 108 Jason Stitt; 110 ER_09; 111 Jackiso; 112br Balazs Justin; 112tl Adisa; 113 imagestalk; 114 Martin Novak; 115 Wiktory; 116 & 184t maragu; 118r Alena Ozerova; 118 Damian Herde; 119 Pakhnyushcha; 120b psnoonan; 120t Vakhrushev Pavel; 121 Liliya Kulianionak; 122 Ronald Sumners; 123 Johanna Goodyear; 124 teekaygee; 125 Subbotina Anna; 126 Dave Allen Photography; 127 Jorg Hackemann; 128 & 132 Tootles; 129 Michelle D Milliman; 130 Baevskiy Dmitry; 131 Carrieanne Larmore; 133 Sarah Salmela; 134 MattJones; 135 Thrithot; 136 guigaamartins; 137 Annette Shaff; 138 Melissa Sue; 140 Sashkin; 141 Studio Barcelona; 142 & 156b imageshunter; 143, 156tl, 242 Liv friis-larsen; 144l kzww; 144r sergojpg; 145 Victoria Alexandrova; 146 Alexey Stiop; 147 Phil Date; 148, 150, 153bl Valua Vitaly; 149 PixAchi; 151 Ienetstan; 152l nastiakru; 152r Penny Hillcrest; 153tr Quayside; 154 Lana K; 155 Irina1977; 157b Ivanova Inga; 157t vgstudio; 158 kristian sekulic; 159 Rick P Lewis; 160 Tania Zbrodko; 161 Kurhan; 162 Alexa Catalin; 164 Jita; 169 Jakub Semeniuk; 172 Tobik; 173 Elena Kharichkina; 174 dionisvera; 175br Goodluz; 175tl Kalim; 176 Vadim Ponomarenko; 177b Leah-Anne Thompson; 177t aspen rock; 178 Ximagination; 179 marilyn barbone; 180 NatalieJean; 181 Stuart Miles; 183b jkitan; 183t AISPIX; 184b Vinicius Tupinamba; 186 Gordon Ball LRPS; 187 librakv; 188, 235 Christopher Elwell; 190l Blaj Gabriel; 190r Selecstock; 191 Noam Armonn; 192 sixninepixels; 193b, 205 Yuri Arcurs; 193t Juri Arcurs; 194 artur gabrysiak; 195 Gorilla; 196 newphotoservice; 197 wavebreakmedia ltd; 199 Aleksandar Todorovic; 200 design56; 201b Piotr Marcinski; 201l Volosina; 201tr Andrei Mihalcea; 202 Volodymyr Burdiak; 203b Faiz Zaki; 203t BeaB; 204l Brooke Becker; 204r kiboka; 206bl Danny Smythe; 206r Kanwarjit Singh Boparai; 207 Robin W; 208 & 212 Vasina Natalia; 209 Wojciech Zbieg; 210 Gaby Kooijman; 211 Zsolt Nyulaszi; 213 James R T Bossert; 214 Ieva Geneviviene; 215 Zholobov Vadim; 216 Donald R. Swartz; 217 inacio pires; 218 & 226t Richard Griffin; 219, 238 Lilyana Vynogradova; 220 Paul Reid; 221 area381; 222 Olga Utlyakova; 223 Lyudmila Mikhailovskaya; 224b Ildi Papp; 224b Jacek Chabraszewski; 226b Mark Plumley; 227b jathys; 227t Marie C Fields; 228b Magdalena Kucova; 228tl B.G. Smith; 229 Tyler Olson; 230t Aleksandra Duda; 231t tacar; 232t Peter zijlstra; 234, 237, 241b Elke Dennis; 236b Gemenacom; 236t buriy; 239 trgowanlock; 245 Elena Veselova; 246b Nataliya Arzamasova; 246t Stephanie Frey; 247r Alex Staroseltsev; 248 Jayme Burrows; 249 Artem Shadrin; 250 Jane Rix; 251 Ingrid Balabanova; 256b Alexander Ruiz Acevedo; 256t kaband.

Household Hints

NATURALLY

Diane & Jon Sutherland,
Maria Costantino, Liz Keevill & Kevin Eyres

FLAME TREE
PUBLISHING

Contents

▦ **Introduction** **6**

▦ **Cleaning & Laundry** **18**

   Cleaning Around the House 20

   Kitchen & Bathroom 46

   Laundry 72

▦ **Home & Garden** **94**

   General Household & Home Improvement 96

   Pests & Garden 116

   Pet Care 128

▦ **Health & Personal Care** **140**

   Beauty Tips 142

   Apple Cider Vinegar 168

   Natural Remedies 172

▦ **Food** **216**

   Culinary Basics 218

▦ **Index** **252**

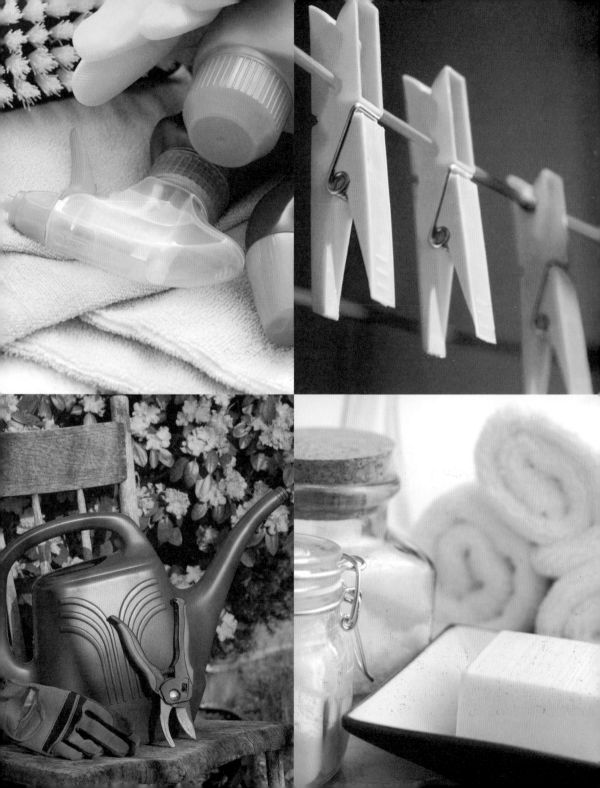

Introduction

Baking Soda

If you could find a naturally occurring product that you could use as a deodorant, a toothpaste, an exfoliant and an antiseptic, you'd be impressed. If you found out that you could use the same substance in the kitchen to make a big improvement to many of your favorite dishes, and then use it to clean out your pots and pans, leaving them grease-free and shining, you'd be amazed. And if you were told that exactly the same product could be used to shampoo your pets, clean out your swimming pool, kill cockroaches and relieve insect bites and stings, you'd probably just laugh. Well, there is just such a product, it's been around for thousands of years in one form or another and you can by it today for pennies.

It All Started in Ancient Egypt

When the ancient Egyptians needed something that would keep mummified bodies dry and free from bacteria on their journey through the afterlife, they found the answer: a sodium compound, occurring naturally in dry lake beds. They called the substance Natron because a particularly good source was an area called Wadi-el-Natrun. The Egyptians quickly discovered that Natron could also be used as an extremely effective cleaner around the home. Not only that, but blended with olive oil it made soap; in its natural state it could be used as toothpaste and diluted it made a breath-freshening antiseptic mouthwash.

What's more, they found that Natron burned with a smokeless flame when mixed with castor oil – handy for working in tombs without leaving soot stains. And it was useful in chemical processes such as glass making. All in all a pretty remarkable and versatile substance.

Then Came Pearlash and Soda Ash

Over the centuries the various elements that make up Natron were refined down to more specific substances for individual uses. Late in the eighteenth century European chemists discovered that another form of sodium, pearlash, was particularly useful in dramatically speeding up the baking process. However, the production of pearlash involved the burning of huge amounts of wood to produce ash, and pretty soon wood for pearlash was in short supply.

In 1791 French chemist Nicolas LeBlanc produced a process for turning common salt (sodium chloride) into soda ash (sodium carbonate), a substance with the same characteristics as pearlash but without the need to burn vast tracts of woodland.

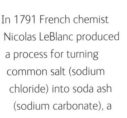

And Finally There Was Baking Soda

American bakers loved soda ash and America was soon producing its own. However, American soda ash couldn't match the quality of the European product so American bakers were forced to import large quantities of European soda ash.

All that changed in the 1830s when an American, Austin Church, began experimenting with new ways of producing high-quality sodium bicarbonate. Church, a doctor,

developed a process that converted purified sodium carbonate into food-grade sodium bicarbonate. Giving up his medical practice, Church joined forces with his brother-in-law, John Dwight, moved to New York, and founded John Dwight & Co. Dwight called his sodium bicarbonate Saleratus (aerated salt) and was soon selling it to bakers and housewives across the States.

Thirty years later Austin Church retired from the business a rich man, but he wasn't finished with sodium bicarbonate. With his two sons he set up Arm & Hammer to produce baking soda products, and if you go into any drugstore or supermarket you can still find Arm & Hammer toothpaste on the shelves.

You Can Call It:

- baking soda
- bread soda
- bicarbonate of soda or 'bicarb' (both more commonly used in the United Kingdom)
- sodium bicarbonate
- saleratus
- or even, **sodium hydrogen carbonate**

But Don't Confuse It with:

- **caustic soda** (sodium hydroxide)
- **baking powder** (although it does contain baking soda)
- **sodium chloride** (common table salt)
- **sodium carbonate** (also known as washing soda, or soda ash)

Vinegar

Vinegar has been made and used for thousands of years: in fact, vinegar is the oldest storable food and because it can be stored for an almost unlimited period, it is the only food without an expiry date.

The ancient Babylonians around 5000 BC were among the first to recognize the versatile nature of vinegar and used it as both a preserver and a condiment. They were also the first to flavor vinegar with herbs and spices. The 'Father of Medicine', Hippocrates (460–370 BC) is known to have prescribed vinegar to his patients in order to restore the four humors (blood, black bile, yellow bile and phlegm) to a balanced harmony. Vinegar is also mentioned in the Bible – in the Book of Ruth and in Proverbs, and it was specified in the Talmud for making *haroseth*, a dried fruit and nut paste eaten at Passover as a reminder of the mortar used in buildings by the Israelites when they were slaves in Egypt.

Medicinal Use Continues

In the nursery rhyme, when 'Jack fell down and broke his crown' he bound his head with vinegar and brown paper. The therapeutic benefits of vinegar have been known for centuries: in Asia, vinegar is known as the 'friend of Chinese herbs' because it is often used in the preparation of traditional medicines. During the American Civil War, vinegar was used to treat scurvy and as recently as the First World War it was being used in trench hospitals to sterilize wounds.

Whether you call them 'traditional', 'natural' or 'folk' remedies or recipes, today vinegar continues to be one of the most versatile products in the kitchen and medicine cabinet. And, with our growing awareness of the impact of chemicals on our environment, vinegar finds itself once more at the forefront of household cleaning.

Production

Vinegar is nothing more than an alcoholic beverage that has 'gone sour', which explains the French origins of the word *vin aigre*, meaning 'sour wine' – although it was not until 1864 that Louis Pasteur made sense of this natural process of fermentation. When alcoholic beverages sour it is because of the action of certain bacteria, known as *acetobacter*, on the alcohol that turns it to acetic acid and water. Other elements, such as the type of fruit or grain from which the alcohol is originally made, give different vinegars their individual characteristic tastes, bodies and colors.

The Orleans Method

In theory, making vinegar is a very simple process: make some wine (or beer) and expose it to the air for the vinegar bacteria to get to work. The *acetobacter* reaction is an aerobic reaction, and simply requires the presence of oxygen. One of the oldest methods for producing vinegar is called the Orleans process. The 'generator' used is a large wooden barrel that is laid on its side with the bung hole facing towards the top. At each end of the barrel, holes are drilled so that when the beer or dilute wine is put in, the liquid in the barrel is just below the holes. The slow fermentation allows for a non-toxic slime known as the 'vinegar mother' composed of the bacteria and soluble cellulose, to form on top of the liquid.

The barrel holes are covered with fine gauze (to keep out insects) and the 'generator' allowed to sit for several months at around 87°F /29°C. When all the liquid is turned to vinegar, all but 15 per cent is drawn off through the bottom of the barrel. What is left behind in the barrel is the vinegar mother that becomes the 'starter' for the next batch of vinegar.

The more oxygen available in the process, the faster the vinegar can be made. So, over the centuries vinegar producers came up with a variety of ways of increasing the amount of oxygen in order to shorten the time taken in the vinegar-making process. Today, commercial vinegar is produced using either a fast or slow method: slow methods are used with traditional vinegars and can take several months. A form of nematode, known as a vinegar eel (Turbatrix aceti), that feeds on the vinegar mother, can occur in some forms of vinegar – in particular, naturally fermenting vinegar – but most manufacturers filter and pasteurize their vinegar before bottling, thereby avoiding any adulteration.

Speedy Methods

The fast methods of vinegar production generally add vinegar mother to the liquid, then introduce air using a turbine or pumping system. Additionally, the generator may be loosely packed with a porous material such as *pommace* (grape pulp after is has been pressed) or beech wood shavings to provide a 'mash' with a greater surface area for the volume of vinegar mother. This method can produce vinegar in 24 to 36 hours.

Activity Levels

The acetic acid concentration of vinegar typically ranges from 4 to 8 per cent by volume for condiment (table) vinegar, though it is usually around the 5 per cent mark. It exists in much higher concentrations for pickling – up to 18 per cent – although in some countries the maximum strength may be less than this as solutions above 10 per cent need careful handling as they are corrosive to the skin.

Types of Vinegar

There are many different types of vinegar. The most basic is white distilled vinegar – colorless and transparent in appearance – which is also sometimes called spirit vinegar. Its stronger concentration of acetic acid makes it a valuable household cleansing agent, and so it is the one most frequently used in this book. There is also malt vinegar, beer vinegar, red and white wine vinegar, champagne vinegar, balsamic vinegar, sherry vinegar, rice vinegar, fruit vinegar, raisin vinegar, date vinegar and *ume* vinegar or *umezu*, made from the Japanese pickled plums *umeboshi*. Another useful vinegar that is occasionally called for in this book, is apple cider vinegar. Made from cider or from an apple must or 'mash', cider vinegar has a strong, acid-sharp flavor at full strength, but when dilute, has a distinctive apple taste. Fast industrial manufacture, which can take as little as 24 hours, often uses concentrated juice from eating or dessert apples with added sugar, rather than traditional Somerset cider apple varieties such as Kingston Black, Morgan Sweet, Sheep's Nose and Yarlington Mill, which are fermented naturally for at least two years. Such cider vinegars are a brownish-yellow color, and are often sold unfiltered and so contain vinegar 'mother', which is thought to be beneficial to our health.

Lemons

The bright yellow lemon, with its unmistakable citrus smell, is hugely versatile. Its value as a preservative and for flavoring has long been recognized, but it also has enormous potential in the home; as a beauty product, for health benefits and as a natural cleaning product. It is possible to use every part of the lemon; the juice is rich in fruit acids and natural sugars and for generations it has been used as a remedy for chills and coughs, as well as to ease sunburn and skin rashes.

The Lemon Tree

The Citrus Limon, or the lemon tree, is an evergreen that was originally native to Asia, and particularly to India, Burma and China. The tree is now grown throughout Europe and many other sub-tropical climates, including Arizona and California in the United States. Its oval, fresh-smelling, yellow fruit is popular around the world. It has the added advantage that it bears fruit all year round, and selective cultivation has created dozens of different varieties.

The lemon tree needs warmth and sunshine, good drainage and regular watering. Cultivated trees are regularly pruned and bees are encouraged, as they are essential to pollinate the flowers.

The Versatile Lemon

Although lemons are used commercially for the production of soft drinks and food flavorings, their use in the home has often been limited to culinary use and for adding to drinks. But tangy lemons, and particularly the juice of the fruit, have so much more to offer than just slicing and dropping into a glass of gin and tonic.

Despite having a somewhat sour taste, lemons are incredibly good for us because they are packed full of Vitamin C, healthy nutrients and fiber. In fact every part of the lemon has something to offer; there are organic acids and lemon oil in the peel, fiber and antioxidants in the pith, antioxidants, vitamins, acids, minerals and lemon oil in the pulp, and salts and limonin in the pips.

The term 'superfood' has been bandied around and, as trends change, various fruits and vegetables are lauded as the next best thing. The humble lemon, however, is consistently unique in its versatility.

Nutrients

Lemons are one of the best sources of Vitamin C and just one lemon a day would provide us with our daily requirement of this nutrient. In addition lemons also contain small amounts of Vitamins B and E, as well small amounts of protein and fats. A medium-sized lemon only contains a tiny amount of sugar, just fifteen calories, plus a number of minerals, including calcium, copper, iron, manganese, magnesium, potassium, phosphorus, selenium and zinc.

In the lemon's fiber there is cellulose that helps absorb water, so it is an excellent diuretic and perfect to deal with constipation and diarrhea. The pectin in the fiber is particularly effective in helping our bodies absorb calcium, reduce the absorption of cholesterol and suppress its production. The antioxidants in a lemon help prevent our cholesterol and body fats from being oxidized by free radicals in the body. Oxidized fats can age the skin, make

us more prone to sunburn and infections, allow the formation of gall stones, give us high blood pressure and affect our eyesight. The lemon is also the only one of the citrus fruits that is capable of protecting our DNA from damage because of its high Vitamin C content.

Beauty Benefits

Every single part of a lemon contains something that can help us in our beauty regime too. We can use the juice to lighten our hair, and moisturize or cleanse our skin. Our nails will benefit from a soak in lemon juice, too. Lemons are also present in massage oils, moisturizers, toners, deodorizers, cleansers and exfoliators.

Invaluable Household Tool

It is not just the health benefits that makes the lemon such an amazing fruit. Lemons are incredibly useful for many household chores too; from freshening the air to cleaning and polishing, to disinfection and stain removal and even dealing with annoying insects. Combining the lemon or its juice with other simple household standbys such as baking soda or salt provides an inexpensive and effective cleaning product.

That Lemony Smell

Lemons have an unmistakeable scent and their distinctive taste comes from the acids they contain. Several other plants have a similar scent, such as lemongrass, lemon verbena or lemon balm and there are also lemon-scented varieties of popular herbs, such as mint, basil and thyme.

We are not just content to use the physical properties of the lemon, but also to make full use of the aroma they provide. That's why the lemon is such a popular additive to so many off-the-shelf cleaning products. There is something unmistakeable, fresh, clean and very appealing about that lemony smell.

Only the Best Will Do

Whether you buy lemons at a market stall, a greengrocer or a large supermarket, you should feel the fruit you are going to buy. Opt for smooth skins because this usually means less peel and more pulp, which means more juice. Sometimes you can tell by the weight; if the lemon is small but quite heavy then it should be full of pulp and juice. Ignore any fruit that has blemishes, or is shriveled or spongy when gently squeezed in the palm of the hand.

Color and Appearance

Choose a deep yellow color lemon that is firm to the touch (but not too hard), not too large at each end and shows no sign of damage. Bruised or damaged lemons will not keep as well because they will be susceptible to mold. A good-quality lemon should feel oily but fine and smooth-skinned.

Waxed or Unwaxed?

With any number of pesticides, fungicides, insecticides, bactericides and preservatives being sprayed during the growing process, the best option is to choose an organic unwaxed lemon. This is particularly important if you intend to

use the lemon peel, as normally organic and unwaxed lemons have had no routine use of pesticides at any stage of the growing or transportation process. This helps to ensure that the peel is untreated and that no pesticide or wax has penetrated the pulp of the lemon. If you are unsure about whether or not the lemon has been waxed, or what it may have been treated with, then washing it well before use will at least remove any substance that has remained on the peel.

Storing

Whole lemons can be kept in a plastic bag in the refrigerator for up to 10 days, or perhaps even longer. It will start to shrivel when it is no longer fresh and the skin of the fruit will take on a pitted look. If you do not have a refrigerator then a cool, dark room is a good substitute. Do not be tempted to freeze a whole lemon, as once it thaws it will probably only be useful for puree, or at best to be chopped. You can freeze the juice and the zest, though. Try filling ice-cube trays with juice so you freeze it with recipe-sized portions. Or to give your ice-cubes a bit of a tangy kick, add a few drops of lemon juice to the water before freezing. Lemon peel can also be stored in a refrigerator in an airtight bag for several days. Or strips of peel can be frozen, as can slices of lemon, or lemon wedges. If you want to store lemon wedges for a few days then cover them in plastic wrap. However if you are saving the lemon wedges for a savory dish, you can preserve them for a few days by coating them in vinegar.

It's All in the Preparation!

If you are using a waxed lemon for cooking, it is advisable to wash it in hot, clean water before beginning your preparation. This is to remove any pesticides that may have been sprayed on the fruit to help preserve it. Alternatively you could fill a basin with freshly boiled water, then submerge the lemon(s) for 30 seconds to dissolve the wax. Whichever method you use, remember to rinse the lemon under cold, running water before beginning your preparation.

Juicing a Lemon

To get the most juice possible out of a stored lemon, remove the fruit from the refrigerator in good time. A lemon at room temperature will provide you with much more juice than one that has been kept cold in the refrigerator. A medium-sized lemon should provide 2–3 tbsp/30–45ml/1–1½ fl oz of juice. Another tip is to either pop the lemon in the microwave for 10 to 15 seconds, or roll the lemon with your hand on the work

surface. Both of these methods help produce more lemon juice, as the pulp's membranes are broken down.

You can squeeze the lemon to obtain juice in a number of different ways. You could use your hands, provided they are big enough and strong enough. Manual lemon squeezers come in glass, metal or plastic. These have a ribbed top and a tray to catch the pips, with a collecting area for the juice you've managed to extract. There are also electric versions of this type of citrus squeezer. You can also buy a 'citrus reamer', which is a wooden, metal or plastic hand-held version of the classic squeezer – you push the conical end into the lemon half and grind out the juice. Then there are also wooden or metal, hand-held lemon squeezers that are often called 'citrus trumpets'. The ribbed top is screwed into the lemon and rotated to obtain the juice, which pours out of the trumpet-shaped end.

Lemon Zest

The zest of a lemon refers only to the bright yellow peel and not the white pith that lines it. The pith is very bitter, although it does have some nutrient value. Zest has a very strong lemon flavor and is an ideal flavoring for many recipes. You can grate the peel using a conventional grater, but choose the finest option and brush the zest off with a pastry brush. A traditional lemon zester can also be used. This cuts long, thin, threadlike strands of zest through its tiny cutting holes. If you do not have a zester or grater, use a vegetable peeler or a small, sharp, paring knife. Carefully peel off a strip of the lemon zest, making sure you only take the yellow layer. If there is any pith showing on the underside of the peel then it is best to remove this.

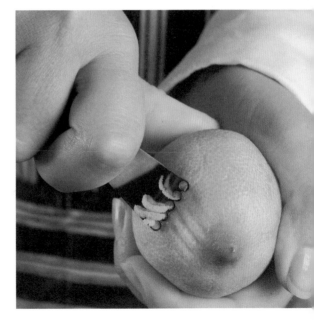

Cleaning & Laundry

Cleaning Around the House

Most detergents and general household cleaning products are expensive and packed with chemicals. Baking soda, lemons and vinegar are natural, organic and environmentally friendly – perfect substitutes for many of these harmful household cleaning products. They are an incredibly useful cleaning resource and can be used for a huge variety of different chores in the home. They cost just a fraction of the price and are so much better for your health.

All-purpose Cleaner

Drain Training

If the water isn't draining away as fast as it normally does, or you suspect you've got a blockage, it's time for action. Pour about 100 g/4 oz/½ cup baking soda down the sink swiftly followed by about 120 ml/4 fl oz/½ cup of white vinegar. Put the plug in while the chemicals froth up in a rather satisfying way. Leave bubbling away for a couple of hours then pour down a few pints of boiling water. Used regularly, this combination will break down the fatty acids that block drains and help to keep them smelling fresh as a daisy.

Going on Vacation?

Don't forget to put a handful of baking soda down all plugholes in the home before you go away for any longer than a couple of days. It'll prevent your neighbors suffering any unpleasant bad drain smells while you're gone, especially in hot weather, and it will make your place much nicer for you to come home to.

Skeptical about Septic Tanks?

If you've got a septic tank, don't worry. Baking soda is best for keeping it in tiptop shape. In fact, it positively helps the process of breaking down waste by keeping the contents at the correct pH level, which favors the right sort of bacteria. Baking soda also helps protect the fabric of the tank from corrosion that can be caused by too-acid an environment. So, if you don't have mains drainage, pop a handful of soda down the toilet each week and give your tank a healthy treat.

Mineral and Limescale Build-up

Lemons are great for removing the build-up of limescale from around stainless steel sinks and draining boards. The lemon peel is also excellent at keeping chrome taps free from limescale. All you have to do is cut a lemon in half and rub it over the affected area. Leave the lemon to do its work for at least a minute and then rinse with cold water and buff with a soft, dry cloth.

CAUTION: Do not use lemon juice or the peel on gold-plated taps and plug holes as this can cause them to tarnish.

Disinfectant

If you want to kill bacteria without having to clean off the residue left by most chemical cleaning products, why not use a lemon? The acids contained in lemon juice kill off the bacteria, which do not survive long in an acidic environment. Lemon juice can disinfect most kitchen worktops, including cutting boards and sinks, as well as bathroom sinks and surfaces. The juice kills the bacteria in a natural way and leaves a fresh fragrance.

Why not try adding a small amount of lemon juice to drinking water to ensure that no bacteria are surviving there?

Remove Candle Wax

Candles give a gorgeous light and scented candles are a wonderful way to perfume a room. Apart from the fire risk, the only other problem with candles is that they can splutter molten wax onto walls and furniture.

Rather than scrape off the wax with a knife or blade, which may damage the surface underneath, heat it gently first with a hair dryer and blot up as much molten wax as you can with paper towels. Next, tackle the greasy marks by mopping them with a clean rag soaked in a solution of equal parts white vinegar and water and then blot with a clean, dry cloth.

Un-stick Stickers

Trying to remove the stuck-on price tags from new china and glassware – or from any other object – is probably one of the most frustrating and time consuming activities on the planet. You can peel, poke, and rub away and still there are bits that will not shift.

Thankfully there is a straightforward method: saturate the sticker with undiluted white vinegar and scrape it off. Do not use your fingernail: it will only break! Try using a plastic knife for small, delicate objects so that you do not scratch the surface, or an expired credit or phone card for larger surfaces.

If there are any sticky leftovers, saturate again with vinegar and wipe clean with a cloth. This method works equally well for those sticky decals that are popular with young children and notices on car windows left by parking meter attendants.

Degreaser

Pure lemon juice is a great way to get rid of a grease build-up – such as on door handles and knobs. You have to apply the juice liberally to the affected area and give it a little time to cut through the grease, but it does work and you also have the added bonus of the fresh smell of lemons. The limonene in the lemon's essential oil is what removes the grease and this also has anti-bacterial properties. A spray of equal parts of water and white vinegar works well too.

Furnishings & Surfaces

Back and White

White painted furniture can quickly lose its original brightness. Bring it up like new by wiping faded items over with a solution of 2 tablespoons baking soda to 1 litre/1¾ pints/1¼ qts warm water. Scrub black marks off chair legs with a paste of baking soda and water. Rinse and dry.

Ring the Changes

Get rid of cup-rings and other heat marks on wooden furniture by gently rubbing with a baking soda and water paste. If this doesn't work, add a pea-sized blob of toothpaste for extra abrasion. Make sure you don't get the furniture wet as this may cause further stains. Wipe over, dry carefully and, finally, buff with some furniture polish.

A wet glass on a wooden table inevitably leaves a white ring mark. These can be removed by a mixture of equal parts vinegar and olive oil and applying it with a soft cloth. Do not rub in circles, but move the cloth along the grain of the wood. Use a second clean cloth to polish up to a shine.

Dry-clean Your Three-piece Suite in Fifteen Minutes

To give any fabric upholstery a quick dry-clean, sprinkle the surfaces generously with baking soda (use a flour shaker or empty talc container). Leave for about 10 or 15 minutes to absorb any stale odors then vacuum up all the powder.

Degrease

Annoying grease marks on cloth upholstery can be made to vanish by sprinkling with one part baking soda and one part salt. Simply brush the mixture in lightly with an old toothbrush then leave overnight to absorb the stain. Vacuum up the next day.

Alternatively ...

Make a paste of 1 tablespoon water and 3 tablespoons baking soda and rub into stains on fabric seat covers – an old toothbrush works well. Leave the mixture to dry then brush carefully with a clean dry brush and vacuum away any residue.

CAUTION: When applying any substance to any upholstery, it is best to test the mixture first on an inconspicuous area to check that the fabric is colorfast and that it won't affect the surface of the fabric or leave water marks.

A Cure for Under-the-weather Leather and Vinyl

Leather and vinyl furniture often has a textured finish that can trap grease and dirt, leading to a generally grimy effect. Revive the finish by mixing 1 tablespoon baking soda with 250 ml/8 fl oz/1 cup warm water and use on a cloth or sponge to wipe down the furniture. Blast more stubborn grime with a paste of baking soda and water. Rubbing this into all the nooks and crannies will leave everything sparkling clean. Wipe over well with clean water on a sponge or cloth and dry.

Unsightly white water marks on leather furniture can also be removed by dabbing them with a sponge dipped in undiluted white vinegar.

Leather that has lost its shine can be revitalized with a mixture of equal parts of white vinegar and boiled linseed oil (available form art shops and hardware stores). Put the solution into a spray bottle and spray onto the leather. Spread it over the surface gently with a soft cloth and give it a minute or so to nourish the leather, then buff with a clean cloth.

Leather-topped tables are best cleaned by wiping with a soft cloth dipped in a solution of 2 parts water and 1 part white vinegar and dried off with a soft, clean cloth.

Metal Furniture

Grimy metal furniture can be brought back to life by cleaning with a paste of baking soda and water on a cloth or sponge. Rinse clean and dry carefully to prevent rust formation.

Rust-buster

If rust does appear on metal furniture, wipe over the affected area with a paste made from 1 tablespoon baking soda and a few drops of water on a damp cloth. Then polish with a piece of baking foil and wipe down with a clean damp cloth and dry carefully with kitchen paper.

Lackluster Laminates?

Any laminate surfaces that are looking a bit off-color will respond well to being spruced up with a damp cloth or sponge sprinkled with baking soda. Rinse and dry.

Furniture Polish

The limonene in the lemon's essential oils can dissolve the different types of grime that build up on wooden furniture. This can include old furniture polish, wax, fingerprints and general dust and dirt. To make your own furniture polish, mix together, in a sealable container so it will keep, 250 ml/8 fl oz/1 cup of olive oil with 120 ml/4 fl oz/½ cup of freshly squeezed and strained lemon juice. You need to strain the lemon juice before mixing it with the olive oil to make sure there are no residual lumps of lemon pulp. Now dab a little of your mixture onto a clean cloth and polish the furniture in the normal way. The lemon juice is great for grime-busting, but the olive oil also gives wooden furniture a lovely shine and nourishes the wood, too. This mixture can also be used for bringing a shine to hardwood floors.

Scratches in Wood

Unsightly scratches on wooden surfaces can be disguised using a little white or apple cider vinegar mixed in a jar with some iodine. Adjust the color to match the wood – more vinegar for light woods, more iodine for dark woods – and paint the scratch mark carefully with an artists' paint brush.

Wax and Polish Build-up

When furniture polish or wax builds up on surfaces you can remove it easily and without damaging the underlying wood with a mixture of equal proportions of white vinegar and water. Dip a cloth into the mix and wring it out well, then, moving in the direction of the grain of the wood clean off the polish. Wipe dry with a soft clean cloth.

Marble and Ivory Surfaces Cleaner

If you have marble worktops, or marble-topped pieces of furniture, you will know that they can become stained and how hard it is to remove those stains. Some people claim lemon can be used – by cutting a lemon in half, dipping it in some salt and using this to scrub the stain.

If you do try this, test first on an inconspicuous area, rub very gently and rinse the lemon juice off the surface swiftly and thoroughly. The same applies to ivory surfaces, such as piano keys or knife handles. To whiten ivory, try rubbing it with lemon juice that has been diluted with an equal amount of water. Apply this mix carefully so that none of the liquid gets into metal parts of a piano, then wipe dry with a clean, soft cloth.

CAUTION: Due to lemon's acidity it is risky to use it on marble, as it can etch into the rock, so you may want to play safe and avoid it entirely, rather than risk expensive repairs. Also, trying to remove the yellowing of antique ivory piano keys may reduce the antique-look and therefore possibly the value of the piano as a whole.

Odor Removal from Wooden Surfaces

Wooden surfaces, like kitchen worktops and cutting boards, can harbor harmful germs and soak up a variety of different food odors. Onions, fish and garlic are good examples of foods that can soak into wood and stay there. Rub half a lemon liberally over the wooden surface. Let the lemon juice dry fully, then rinse it off with cold water. This will disinfect the surface and remove all those unpleasant odors.

Wooden furniture can also harbor smells, such as pet 'deposits' and stale tobacco. Rubbing with half a lemon can help remove the odors.

If your wooden furniture has drawers, then you can try placing a small dish of baking soda mixed with lemon juice inside a drawer. This will help to neutralize any lingering smells.

Floors & Walls

All Floors

Looking for an excellent general-purpose hard-floor cleaner that costs pennies? Try dissolving a handful of baking soda in a bucket of warm water and use as normal on a floor mop. Wring out well to avoid saturating the surfaces, then stand back and admire the finish.

Good for Wood

Water can damage parquet and other solid wooden floorings. To remove any offending water marks take a damp cloth or sponge and sprinkle a little baking soda onto it then rub carefully. Wipe over with a well wrung-out cloth or sponge and dry carefully.

CAUTION: Don't get the floor wet as this will obviously cause further problems.

Lifeless Lino, Vinyl or Cork Flooring?

Unsightly scuff marks from dark shoe soles on lino, vinyl flooring and cork tiles will vanish when rubbed with a paste of baking soda and water.

Bring the shine back to a vinyl floor without making it slippery by washing it with a solution of 120 ml/4 fl oz/½ cup of white vinegar to each 4-litre/gallon bucket of water. Many stains can be safely removed from linoleum floor covering by applying a splash of white vinegar, sprinkling baking soda on top and rubbing gently. Rinse clean with water afterwards.

Crying Over Spilt Ink?

It's no use crying over spilt ink – you just have to do something about it. For spills on hard surfaces, wipe up as much ink as possible then sprinkle with baking soda. Leave for a few minutes to absorb any residue, then add more powder and rub at the stain with a wet cloth or sponge. For really stubborn stains, moisten the powder with a little vinegar instead of water.

This Works on all Floor Types

Most types of floors can be cleaned effectively by combining lemon oil with other natural products. For a simple mix, add 4 tbsp of white vinegar to a bucket of hot water. Then add 10 drops of lemon oil before mopping the floor as normal.

Ceramic tiled floors, as well as hardwood and laminate floors, can also be cleaned using a combination of lemon oil, water, white vinegar and your own choice of two more essential oils, for example tea-tree oil

and lavender, geranium or bergamot. To create this great-smelling and effective floor cleaner, mix together 250 ml/8 fl oz/1 cup of both white vinegar and water. Then add five drops each of the lemon oil and your choice of two other essential oils. You can use a spray bottle to lightly apply the mixture to the floor before mopping or wiping with a clean, preferably lint-free cloth.

On the Carpet

The sooner you deal with any stain, the better your chance of successfully removing it. This applies just as much to carpets as anything else. If you spill wine or drop grease on your favorite Axminster, sprinkle the area with baking soda (or one part baking soda and one part salt), brush in gently and leave it to absorb the stain for several hours. Sweep up the powder with a clean brush then dab with a solution of baking soda and warm water. Leave to dry completely, then vacuum the area.

Some carpet stains can be removed with a paste made from 2 tablespoons white vinegar and 4 tablespoons baking soda or ordinary cooking salt. Test on an inconspicuous part of the carpet first for color fastness, and if it is safe, gently work the paste into the stained area: do not rub outwards as this will spread the stain, instead work from the edge of the stain towards the middle. Let the paste dry and the next day vacuum or brush up the powder residue.

Vacuuming

If you're going to vacuum the carpet, it will be much fresher afterwards if you sprinkle it with baking soda first. Leave it for about 10–15 minutes, or better still overnight, to work, then vacuum the carpet until all traces of powder have disappeared.

Preventative Strike

Before having a new carpet laid, vacuum the bare floor carefully, then sprinkle it all over with baking soda to help keep your carpet smelling fresh. Make sure you tell the fitters not to sweep up the powder, though.

That's Sick

Cleaning up vomit is never a pleasant job but bring baking soda to the rescue and you can ensure there are no lingering nasty memories. Get your rubber gloves on (sprinkling a little baking soda inside them for freshness and ease of removal) and scrape up as much mess as possible, then cover the area with a layer of baking soda. Leave for a few minutes, then scrub from the edges towards the middle with a sponge or brush moistened repeatedly in clean warm water. Sprinkle the area again with baking soda and leave to dry, then vacuum up the powder.

The antibacterial action of baking soda will deal with any residual odors, even on carpet. This process also works well with urine.

If you can't clear up vomit immediately because you're in the middle of an emergency, throw some baking soda over the affected area to curb nasty smells and deal with it as soon as possible.

Removing 'Artwork' from Walls

To clean marks, such as those from crayon, pencil, marker pens or grease, off washable walls, make a solution of baking soda and warm water and wipe over. If any children's masterpieces or other stains prove hard to shift, sprinkle dry baking soda on a damp cloth or sponge and scour gently. It's a good idea to test out on an inconspicuous area of wall first, just in case the finish isn't as washable as you thought.

Washable Wallpaper

Rub stains on washable wallpaper with a paste of baking soda mixed with a little water. However, bear in mind there is washable and washable, so in case your paper is 'wipeable' rather than 'scrubbable', always test on a less noticeable part of the wall first.

Revive Dull Tiles

Wipe dull, lifeless tiles over with a solution of baking soda, and see them spring back to their old shiny selves. Use the powder dry on a wet cloth or sponge for more stubborn stains and to clear soap residue. When you've finished, rinse with clear water and wipe or squeegee dry.

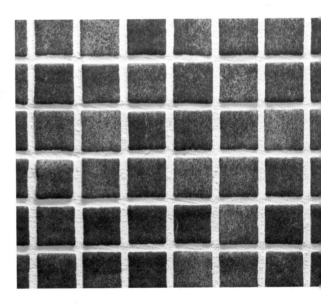

Defeat Grubby Grouting

Grubby grouting will never show your bathroom in its best light. Revive stained tile grout with a thick paste of baking soda and an old toothbrush. Make sure you rinse the whole area clean when you've finished to remove any white streaks.

Alternatively, for general discoloration on tile grout, make up a fizzy paste using two parts baking soda and one part vinegar or lemon juice. Apply the paste to the grout with a toothbrush (not one you're currently using), leave for 10 minutes and then rinse the whole lot off with warm water.

If your grout has really stubborn stains that simply refuse to budge, it's time to use a big gun. Moisten the baking soda with bleach instead of water (but not more than one part bleach to three parts baking soda) and scrub the grout with this, rinsing well afterwards and wiping.

CAUTION: If you do decide to use the bleach mixture as a last resort, you'll need to take a few simple precautions: open the window and wear rubber gloves and old clothes, wash any splashes off your skin immediately, keep the mixture away from children and pets and, of course, make sure you dispose of any leftover mixture safely.

Windows

Let There Be Light

This is the tried and trusted method for getting windows (and mirrors) squeaky clean – it is also cheap and it keeps flies away too! Mix up equal parts of water and white vinegar in a spray bottle. Spray onto the glass and clean off the dirt with scrunched up newspaper. Finish off with a light polish with some brown paper.

Paint Splashes on Windows

Dribbles of dried-on paint on windows look very unsightly but can be hard to remove without scratching the glass. The easy solution is to 'paint' on undiluted hot white vinegar onto the mark and give the died-on paint time to soften up before scraping off carefully with a razor-edged tool.

First Class Glass

For a more thorough clean using baking soda too, wash your windows regularly with a wet cloth or sponge sprinkled with a little baking soda. Rinse over with clean water and polish with a crumpled sheet of newspaper until dry, which will help remove any water marks or smears. And don't forget the frames. Wipe them down with a mixture of one part vinegar to two parts baking soda. This is especially effective if condensation has left areas of mildew.

Mirror, Mirror on the Wall

Like windows, mirrors can quickly loose their luster. Baking soda is great for bringing up grubby mirrors so they gleam. See yourself in a new light by sprinkling a little baking soda on a damp sponge or cloth and rubbing over the mirror. Wipe over with a clean cloth or sponge and fresh water, then polish with a crumpled newspaper for a sparkling, smear-free finish.

Lemon Luster

Wedges of lemon can be rubbed over windows and mirrors to effectively clean and shine them. Squeeze the wedge of lemon as you rub to release some of the lemon juice then wipe the glass with a dampened cloth immediately. Then buff with a clean, dry cloth to produce the shine.

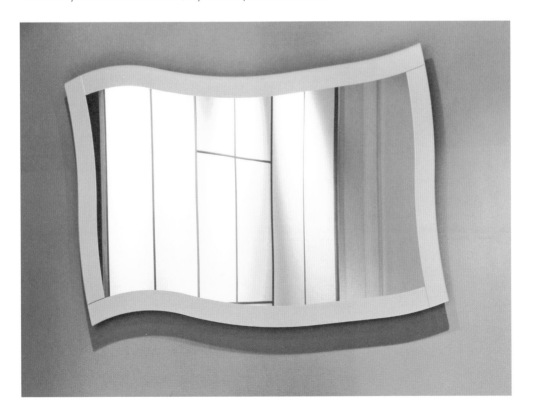

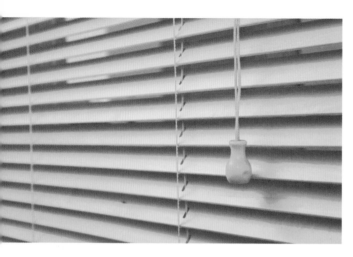

Beautiful Blinds

The horizontal slats of plastic or wooden Venetian blinds are notorious for collecting dirt, dust and grime. Wearing a cotton glove – or even an old sports sock placed over your hand – moistened at the end with a solution of equal parts white vinegar and warm water, run your hand across both sides of the blind slats to clean. You will be amazed at how much dirt is removed, so periodically you will have to rinse out the glove.

Washable blinds (do make sure they are washable) will come back to their just-bought glory once you've doused them in a bath of warm water and 250 ml/8 fl oz/1 cup baking soda. Wipe away the dirt with a sponge or dishwashing brush (give the cords a quick scrub too), then rinse down using the shower head or take outside and give a gentle blast with the garden hose. Hang the blind up to dry.

CAUTION: Place an old towel in the bottom of the bath first to prevent the blind scratching or marking it.

Metal Cleaning

All-Purpose Metal Cleaner

Go to the household store and you will find an expensive array of different scourers, polishes and cleaners labeled for chrome, steel or copper. There is no need to spend money on different products when you can make an effective all-round metal cleaner yourself for a few pennies – and be safe in the knowledge that you are not harming the environment.

Mix a tablespoon of ordinary cooking salt and flour (self rising or plain!) with a little white vinegar to make a paste. Work the paste around the surface to be cleaned then rinse with warm water.

Silver Lining

Stop using unpleasant chemicals on your silverware. Instead, banish tarnish by applying a paste of water and baking soda, or dry baking soda on a damp cloth or sponge. Rinse or wipe with clean water and dry. Adding a tiny squeeze of mild detergent or shampoo to the baking soda paste when you're cleaning the family silver will give you even more cleaning power. Rub, rinse and polish dry.

If you're lucky enough to have some large, flat pieces of silverware, cut a potato in half and dip into a tub of baking soda. Rub over the surface of the silver then polish clean with a soft cloth.

The Family Jewels

You can clean several small items of solid silver jewelry together by placing them in a suitably sized flat glass dish lined with a piece of slightly scrunched-up aluminum foil or baking foil. Arrange the jewelry on the foil, ensuring each piece is in contact with it. Sprinkle the pieces with baking soda. Then boil a kettle of water, let it cool slightly and pour over the items until they are all submerged. Turn the items over gently so all surfaces are in contact with the foil in turn. The tarnish will transfer to the foil. Magic.

Rings can get clogged up and grimy from daily contact with oily deposits from skin, hand cream, soap or other cosmetics. Bring your precious jewels back to pristine condition by soaking them in a solution made from 1 tablespoon baking soda thoroughly mixed with a cup of tepid water.

CAUTION: Don't use this method on pearls, or jewelry where the gems may be glued in place rather than set in claws. If in doubt about submerging jewelry, rub gently with a baking soda paste using an old, soft toothbrush. Rinse and dry carefully before putting away.

Cleaner for Gold Jewelry

There is no need for expensive cleaners, just submerge gold jewelry in apple cider vinegar for 10 minutes, then rinse off and dry. Note: this is only suitable for plain gold items, not jewelry set with gemstones!

Get Stainless Steel and Chrome Really Stainless

Bring any stainless steel and chrome surfaces back to life with a sprinkle of baking soda on a damp cloth or sponge. If you've got 'brushed' stainless steel surfaces, these have a grain so be sure to rub in the right direction. Wipe away any residues with a clean damp cloth and buff up to a good-as-new shine with a dry cloth.

Brassed off with Your Metalware?

Bring copper, brass or bronze ornaments and door furniture up like new by mixing three parts baking soda and one part lemon juice or white vinegar and cleaning with a soft cloth. But remember that if you're polishing brass, you must make sure it is uncoated or it won't work. You can also try a mixture of 2 tablespoons tomato ketchup and 1 tablespoon white vinegar.

Tarnished Copper, Aluminum and Brass Pans

You know how pots and pans can get tarnished so quickly, particularly copper-bottomed ones? Well, it is not necessary to stand and polish them for hours with a proprietary product if you've got lemons and salt to hand. In fact it isn't restricted to just salt, as you could also dip half a lemon into some baking soda. Salt and baking soda are mild abrasives and the acid in the lemon dissolves the tarnish. Rinse with cold water and buff with a dry, soft cloth to bring back the shine.

You can also make a paste to coat a badly tarnished copper or brass pan. Mix together 50 ml/2 fl oz/¼ cup of ordinary table salt and moisten it with enough lemon juice to make a firm paste. Leave the mix for 10 minutes and then spread it onto your tarnished pots and pans. Then just rinse the item in ordinary, warm tap water and dry with a clean, dry cloth. You can repeat this any number of times without damaging the pot.

Lemon Metal Cleaner

You can clean metal by first dissolving some salt in hot lemon juice (for the juice of one lemon use one tablespoon of salt) and then applying the mixture with a cloth to the item. Rinse well and dry with a clean, soft cloth.

Alternatively, soak a clean cloth in lemon juice and then dip it into some salt before rubbing on the metal. Or if you don't want to use a cloth, you can cut a lemon in half before dipping it into the salt and applying it directly to the metal item. Whichever method you choose, make sure you rinse the item well and then dry with a clean cloth.

Odor Removal

Whiffy Carpets?

Carpets and rugs can get very musty, especially if you have pets. The solution is to sprinkle with baking soda the night before you vacuum. Sleep sound in the knowledge that the baking soda is hard at work absorbing smells. Vacuum as normal the next day.

Get It off Your Chest

Some people like that evocative Lion-the-Witch-and-the-Wardrobe smell that comes from old wooden furniture, but no one likes the way the smell can transfer to clothes, making them feel less than fresh. Banish the smell to Narnia by sprinkling some baking soda in the bottom of the piece of furniture, leave it overnight and vacuum out in the morning, then sprinkle in a bit more and place clean paper over the top.

Banish that dreadful smell of decaying mothballs that hangs about in some ancient furniture by filling a pomander with baking soda, or equal quantities of baking soda and borax, and hanging it up in the wardrobe.

Alternatively ...

If you're feeling creative, or short of cash, make a sachet from old clean tights, or fill a small container and stand it in the corner of the cupboard. Well-washed plastic food containers, or small sturdy cardboard boxes with holes punched in the lid, filled with baking soda are ideal. Having a lid makes it less likely to get tipped over and spilt.

Blanket Measures

If blankets smell musty when you take them out of storage, sprinkle them with baking soda and fold them up. Leave them overnight then shake out in the garden and hang in the sunshine, or give them a 20-minute twirl in the tumble dryer on a low setting.

A Bed of Roses

Mattresses can get fusty, especially if not used for a while – not a pleasant place to lay your head. Get rid of the fug by removing the mattress cover if there is one, dusting the mattress with baking soda and leaving it overnight before vacuuming it up. Turn the mattress over and repeat the process. Add a further sprinkling of baking soda before you put back the mattress cover (it goes without saying you've washed it!) and make up the bed. Pillows will benefit from the same treatment.

Butt Out

If you insist on smoking in spite of everything you're told about it, sprinkling a layer of dry baking soda in your ashtrays offers a double whammy. Not only does it absorb unpleasant smoky odors, but it also works as a fire-extinguisher, so helps put smoldering butts out. Unfortunately it won't do anything about cleaning up your lungs.

Fusty Footwear

Let's face it, trainers, shoes, boots and slippers can start to smell horrible if not taken care of properly. Avoid embarrassing stink-foot by sprinkling a couple of tablespoons of baking soda into each shoe and shaking carefully to distribute throughout its whole length. Tip down the toilet before wearing (the powder, that is, not the shoes) to keep your toilet smelling fresh as well.

For a potentially less messy solution, make sachets to go in your shoes to keep them fresh. The simplest way is to pour some baking soda into the foot section of old tights, knot at the ankle and trim. Pop one in each shoe when you're not wearing them. Sprinkling a bit of baking soda on your feet (and in your socks) before you put your shoes on will help deal with footwear odor at the source if you are prone to this problem.

Most sports shoes are machine washable, so before you put them in the machine, soak them for a few minutes in a bucket with a solution of equal parts white vinegar and water. This will deodorize them and kill any bacteria that have taken up residence. Do the same for sports socks too, and check out the Health & Personal Care section for advice on 'fungal feet' to break the vicious cycle of foot odor.

Game, Set and ... Smell

Sports and swimming bags can smell truly ghastly if they're not kept aired and free of dirty or wet kit. Avoid the shame of stinky kit-bagitis by sprinkling the inside of the emptied bag with baking soda. Leave it overnight then vacuum out. Sprinkle a bit more in the bottom and leave it there to absorb moisture and bad odors.

And if you're a member of a sports club with your own locker, it will stay fresh and much more civilized if you pop a small open container of baking soda in the corner.

Upstairs, Downstairs

Attics, basements and cellars often have a characteristically damp, fusty smell. Tights to the rescue again: cut the legs off and fill the foot section with baking soda. Add another layer of tights to make double thickness, and then knot firmly. Use the rest of the leg to make a loop and attach it to a rafter, beam or hook. It might look odd (actually, it does look odd) but it does the trick.

Love Your Luggage

Suitcases, trunks, travel bags and other items of luggage often get stored for months at a time and can get a musty smell, especially when left in the loft or attic. When you get your luggage down for a trip, sprinkle a little baking soda inside the day before you pack, leave overnight and vacuum thoroughly in the morning.

If spots of mildew appear on superior-looking leather luggage that's been left in storage or damp conditions, bring it back to its rightful position in life by gently rubbing the affected areas with a paste of baking soda and water. Dry off with a clean cloth, leave to dry thoroughly, then buff up with a suitable colored polish.

Tame that Tome

Old books can be yet another source of unpleasant musty odors. Use an old librarian's trick once you're sure the book is dry, and sprinkle lightly throughout with baking soda. Leave the book for a few days then shake out the powder. The result: a book it's a pleasure to get your nose stuck into again.

Accidental water spills can cause the pages of books to buckle and stick together, but don't despair. Dry out wetness (or dampness) on paper by sprinkling the affected pages with baking soda and leave the book to dry in a sunny window or the airing cupboard, turning the pages regularly.

Smoke and Cooking Smells

Burned your dinner? Fried some fish? Had a great party? Banish lingering smells by placing bowls of neat white vinegar around the house. Smells will disappear in a day. Clear cigarette smoke from the air by flapping a tea towel moistened in white vinegar around the room! Preparing fish and strong smelling produce like garlic and onions can leave your hands – and food preparation surfaces – smelly. White vinegar will remove the odors from surfaces, but before you handle fish or cut vegetables, try wiping your hands with vinegar first, it will make it easier to remove the odor afterwards.

Freshen Closets

A musty smelling closet needs cleaning and airing out – otherwise your clothes will smell the same! Take out all the contents of your closet, and then, wearing rubber gloves to protect your skin, wash down the walls, ceiling and floor with a cloth dampened in a solution of 120 ml/4 fl oz/½ cup white vinegar, 120 ml/4 fl oz/½ cup ammonia and 4 tablespoons baking soda mixed in a bucket with 4 litres/1 gallon of water. Let the closet dry out completely before returning the contents.

If a smell persists, try placing a box of clean cat litter on the floor to absorb the scent – and any residual moisture – and replenish every couple of days until the odor has disappeared.

Missing the Point

Vinegar breaks down uric acid so is a great way to deal with little accidents. Clean, disinfect and deodorize urine-splashed surfaces with a solution of equal parts white vinegar and water. Then sprinkle the area with baking soda and let it dry. Brush or vacuum the powder residue after it is dry to the touch.

Look What the Cat Dragged In

If Kitty has been hunting and brought home a mouse, clean the area thoroughly with neat white vinegar after you have retrieved the mouse remains. If it smells a little 'mousey' still, a neat trick is to lay a paper towel on the spot and put a dollop of dishwashing liquid, shower gel or even shampoo on it.

Kitchen & Bathroom

Our kitchens and bathrooms can harbor any
number of unpleasant bacteria and odors. Lemons
and vinegar are good at disinfecting, cleaning and
removing lingering smells, so they are the ideal,
natural way to keep kitchen appliances and bathroom
surfaces fresh and germ free. Baking soda comes into
its own when combatting odor and in combination as
a great cleaner. Read on and see what can be done
for for refrigerators, dishwashers and other appliances
and utensils too.

Washing the Dishes

End that Sinking Feeling

For effective, ecofriendly dishwashing, simply add 1 tablespoon baking soda to a sinkful of hot water and swish in the juice of half a lemon. If you use commercial dishwashing liquid, add a couple of tablespoons (or more) of baking soda to the water to boost its action. This is really effective when dealing with greasy dishes.

A Handy Stand-by

Keep a little bowl of dry soda close to the sink. If you encounter a stubborn stain, dip your dish cloth, brush or sponge in and scrub – the offending mark will be gone in a jiffy. This doesn't just work on crockery and pans but is also great for glass and plastic cookware. But don't use on non-stick finishes though – not ever, never.

And Here's Another One

Pop some baking soda into a flour or sugar shaker and keep it by the sink. Use it to sprinkle on stains, then scrub and rinse. Or recycle a plastic scouring powder or talcum powder container and use to hold dry baking soda. Whatever sort of container you use, be sure to label it carefully so it doesn't get mistaken for food.

Banish Dirty Dishcloths and Washed-up Sponges

Rinse dishcloths and sponges after use in a solution of hot water and baking soda to keep them smelling like roses. Occasionally soak overnight for an extra powerful freshen-up. Always dry cloths thoroughly before putting away to keep them hygienic and to avoid the build-up of unpleasant smells.

Up to Your Elbows in Hot Water?

Keep those Marigolds smelling like daisies by sprinkling a little baking soda into your rubber gloves each time you take them off. Not only will it absorb any dampness and keep them fresh for next time, they will also glide on and off like a dream.

In the Dishwasher

Why spend money on multicolored tablets with a ball stuck in the middle for no apparent reason? Make up your own dishwasher powder by putting 2 tablespoons baking soda and 2 tablespoons borax into the powder compartment for a full load.

What Is that Smell?

To freshen up a whiffy dishwasher and give it a thorough clean, sprinkle about 150 g/5 oz/¾ cup baking soda into the bottom of the machine and run it empty through a complete hot cycle. Whiffiness over.

And reduce odor build-up between cycles by sprinkling about a handful of soda over the dirty dishes and onto the bottom of your dishwasher.

No one wants to return to a smelly dishwasher after they've been on vacation, so sprinkle a little baking soda into the empty machine and leave the door slightly open. It will be a delight to come back to.

Pots and Pans

For those boring things that won't go in the dishwasher, mix together equal quantities of baking soda, borax and salt, and use as a scouring powder that will cut through the heaviest grease and grime on pans, broilers and baking sheets.

Remember to rinse well afterwards, and don't use on non-stick surfaces, such as Teflon, as it will damage them. Soda will also tend to make aluminum pans go darker.

Don't Want to Wash Them Right Now?

Alternatively, soak dirty pots and pans in a basin of hot water with 2 or 3 tablespoons baking soda for about an hour. Then scrub them clean with an abrasive scrubber. Again not for non-stick, under any circumstances.

Left a Pan on the Heat and Forgotten About It?

To remove seriously burned-on food, soak the pan in baking soda and water for 10 minutes before washing. Or scrub the pot with dry soda and a moist scouring pad. Don't use abrasive cleaners on non-stick housewares.

For a really scorched pan with burned-on food in the bottom, scrape off as much of the debris as you can, then pour a thick layer of baking soda directly into the pan. Moisten the baking soda with a little water, then leave to work overnight. This should loosen the burnt food and you'll just need to scrub clean and rinse. If this still doesn't work, boil a strong solution of soda in the pan for about 10 minutes. This should soften up the burnt food sufficiently for you to scrub it away with some dry soda on a damp scourer.

What About Non-stick?

For burnt pans that you don't want to scrub, such as non-stick, bring a mixture of water and 250 ml/8 fl oz/1 cup vinegar to a boil in the pan. Remove from the heat and add a couple of tablespoons of soda. Leave to soak overnight then wipe clean and rinse well.

Give Cutting Board Smells the Chop

Cutting boards can acquire a less-than-pleasant smell over time, so give yours a regular spring clean by shaking over about three tablespoons of baking soda and sprinkling with just enough water to moisten. Leave for about 15 minutes to absorb those onion and garlic odors, then rub well with a wet sponge. Rinse in clean water and allow to dry.

Vinegar is effective against harmful bugs such as E. Coli, Salmonella and Staphylococcus, so clean down wooden and plastic cutting boards, butcher blocks and non-marble counter tops where food preparation takes place with undiluted white vinegar before and after use.

Clean Dirty Dishes

If your dishes need a really good scrub, don't reach for the pan scourers, reach for a lemon. Make a paste with lemon juice, white vinegar and baking soda to scour away the stains on your dishes. Use 1 tsp of white vinegar, 50 ml/2 fl oz/¼ cup of baking soda and squeeze in the juice of half a lemon to scrub away those stains.

Alternatively, dip half a lemon into baking soda and use this to do the scouring. It is equally effective at removing stains from dishes. Although with a little forethought you could pour neat lemon juice onto any baked-on stain and let the dish soak for 10 or 15 minutes. When you come to wash the dish it will be much easier, as the acid in the lemon will have helped to dissolve the baked-on stain. Then you probably won't need to scrub at all!

Mugs and Cups

Use a paste of baking soda and water to remove tea and coffee stains from ceramic and melamine cups. Leave the solution in the cup for a while, then rub and rinse. So much more ecological than bleach, and it doesn't leave an aftertaste.

Clean Discolored Kitchen Utensils

Stainless steel, wooden or plastic kitchen utensils can all benefit from the lemon treatment. Wooden and plastic ones in particular can become discolored and stained. Use the paste you used to clean the dirty dishes to clean them too.

To buff up stainless steel utensils use neat lemon juice mixed with a little salt as your polishing agent. Apply the mixture liberally and then rinse off before buffing with a clean, dry cloth. You'll be amazed at how shiny the lemon juice makes your kitchen utensils look.

Clean China and Glass

Make your dinner service sparkle by adding a splash of white vinegar to your rinse water or dishwasher. Cloudy glasses can be made clear again if you soak them for 10–15 minutes in a solution of equal parts hot water and white vinegar and scrub with a soft bottle brush.

Tea- and coffee-stained cups and mugs can be restored by scrubbing with equal parts vinegar and salt followed by a rinse in warm water.

Clean Discolored Containers

Lemons and the sun are the answer for making your discolored plastic boxes and containers look like new. If your plastic boxes have become discolored inside then rub half a lemon over their inside surface. Make sure you do this on a nice sunny day and let the container sit in full sunlight for as long as possible. The lemon's mild bleaching properties combined with the sun's ability to whiten make this combination a really effective stain remover. You can use it on plastic kitchen utensils, too.

Remove Soft Cheese or Sticky Foods from a Grater

Do you ever use recipes that involve grating sticky foods, such as soft cheese, and you have to try to poke out all the bits that are stuck in the holes of the grater? Well, lemon pulp is the answer. Rub half a lemon over both sides of the grater when you've finished preparing your food and this will easily get rid of the residue. Rinse it when you've finished to watch the bits float away down the plughole.

Broiler Pans

It is the grease that has dripped from food into the broiler pan that smells when you next heat the broiler up. Too much accumulated grease in a broiler pan can also catch fire! Lining the pan with cooking foil is one way of keeping an eye on things, but even then you still need to clean out the pan to get rid of spill, splatters, odors and bacteria. A solution of equal parts of white vinegar and warm water should do the job, but for really greasy pans, use neat vinegar or make a paste of vinegar and salt or baking soda and get scrubbing.

Can Openers

Ever looked really close at the sharp point of the opener or at the cogged wheel? Be horrified at the amount of gunk that is lurking there! Every time you open a can some of that gunk will end up deposited on the surface of the food inside the can! Clean and disinfect your can opener by immersing it in undiluted white vinegar and scrubbing the mechanism with a re-cycled toothbrush.

Surfaces

Work on those Worktops

Wipe your kitchen worktops over with a little dry baking soda sprinkled onto a damp cloth or sponge. Rinse with clean water and wipe dry. It's a safe and natural way to keep surfaces clean and leaves them free of taint.

Alternatively, mix up a solution of baking soda and hot water and use this to wash down your worktops leaving them sparkling and fresh. Rinse and dry as above. Rinse your cleaning cloths or sponges in the same solution and dry thoroughly before putting away.

Remove Berry Stains from Your Worktops

If any berry juice dribbles onto your kitchen work surface lemon juice will remove those stains, too. Pour some freshly squeezed lemon juice onto the stain, then sprinkle some baking soda over it. Let this combination do its job for about an hour before gently scrubbing the stain. Then you can rinse the clean work surface.

Freshen up Formica

To erase stains on laminate worktops such as Formica, use a thick paste of baking soda and rub gently until the offending mark disappears. Rinse well to remove the white residue. If that doesn't fix it, squeeze some lemon juice onto the stain, leave for around half an hour, then add a little dry soda to the lemon. Rub with a sponge, rinse clean and dry.

Kitchen Cabinet Cleaner

Sticky, greasy fingers are usually the culprits when our kitchen cabinet doors look messy. To get rid of the grease and make your cabinets look like new, just make a solution of lemon juice and hot water. Use about 50 ml/2 fl oz/¼ cup of freshly squeezed lemon juice and 250 ml/8 fl oz/1 cup of hot water. Stir the solution and simply wipe onto your cabinets with a clean cloth.

Shining Sinks

Sinks come up sparkling and bright when you clean them with baking soda. Use dry on a damp cloth, or make up a paste with soda and water, and use like cream cleaner.

Because lemons have a mild bleaching property they are great for removing stains on kitchen and bathroom sinks. As well as being a bleaching agent, lemon is also capable of dissolving soap scum and limescale, and it disinfects into the bargain. So there are several handy uses in one natural product.

It is the acid in the lemon that is very effective in getting rid of soap scum build-up. Use neat lemon juice and a sponge to coat the soap scum. Leave it for a few hours to do its work and then rinse with cold water.

Rub half a lemon over your draining boards and taps, then rinse and dry with a clean cloth. This will disinfect and break down any limescale build-up. Lemon juice is a great way to rid your kitchen of a smelly sink!

Back to White

If your porcelain or white enamel sink has taken on an unpleasant yellowish tinge, get it looking like new by mixing 1 liter warm water with 50 g/2 oz/¼ cup soda and 120 ml/4 fl oz/½ cup chlorine bleach. Pour into the sink and leave to soak for a quarter of an hour. Keep children and pets away while you are doing this. Then rinse well until the bleachy smell goes completely.

Degrease Lightning

Prevent the build-up of grease in your kitchen sink drain by regularly putting a large handful of dry baking soda down. Do this about once a month for best results, and make sure you do it just before you set off on vacation so there are no nasty drain smells on your return.

Alternatively ...

Keep your sink drain fresh by regularly putting a handful of baking soda down the plug with the same amount of salt, and follow it down with a cupful of boiling water. Leave for about half an hour, then pour down a whole kettleful of boiling water.

Dispense with Dirty Waste Disposals

Keep waste disposal units clean by switching the unit on and running hot water through it. While it is still running, add a handful of soda, then keep the tap running until all traces of powder have disappeared.

Alternatively, put lemon peel through the unit regularly and rinse with water. It's as easy as that!

Appliances

Top Stove-top Tip

Make a paste of soda and water and use like cream cleaner on a sponge or cloth. Wipe over well to remove all white streaks and rinse with clean water. Alternatively, dampen the stove top thoroughly and sprinkle with baking soda. Leave for half an hour to absorb any grease, then rub clean with a sponge or cloth and rinse well. Wipe over glass stoves with a solution of hot water and baking soda on a sponge or cloth. Tackle any stubborn marks or burned-on food with dry baking soda on a wet cloth.

Lemon juice is well known for its natural cleaning powers, but when mixed with baking soda it is a potent mix. Mix together some baking soda, lemon juice and warm water and spread this paste over the stove top. The baking soda is a mild abrasive and the lemon juice has great degreasing properties. Rinse well to make sure the surface does not remain powdery and buff dry with a clean cloth.

Detox Your Oven Cleaner and Your Oven

Proprietary oven cleaners can be highly toxic, and often contain caustic chemicals that give off dangerous fumes. Not nice. However dirty your oven is inside, baking soda can beat the burned-on grime. Scrape off as much gunge as you can, then mix plenty of baking soda with a little water to make a thick paste. Spread this over the sides and bottom of the cold oven and leave overnight. Wipe down the next day with hot water and repeat if necessary. Use dry baking soda on a scourer or sponge to deal with really stubborn areas, rinsing well afterwards.

You can use a baking soda and lemon juice mix inside the oven too. Because lemons contain natural lemon oil and acid they boost the cleaning process by dissolving grease.

Make sure the oven is completely cool before you apply the lemony baking soda paste. Good proportions to make the ideal paste are 2 tbsp of baking soda to 250 ml/8 fl oz/1 cup of water. To this mix add the juice of a whole lemon. You'll have a clean oven and a fresh smelling kitchen too.

Oven Spritzer

Another way to keep ovens fresh and clean is to spray the interior of the oven with water (a plant or laundry sprayer works well for this), then sprinkle with dry baking soda. Spray again to dampen the powder. Give further spritzes with water every hour or so, leave the mixture overnight and then remove with a cloth. Rinse with hot water.

Can't See through that See-through Door?

Glass oven doors can get so splattered with grease and grime that you can't see through them anymore. Get them crystal clear again by scrubbing with baking soda on a damp cloth or sponge. Rinse well and dry.

Microwave Maxi Cleaning

Insides of microwaves can get sprayed with over enthusiastically heated food leaving them smelling musty, especially when the door is kept closed. To refresh your microwave without leaving any taint or chemical smells, remove the turntable plate if there is one, and wash this in the sink in a solution of hot water and baking soda, then dry.

Wipe over the inside of the microwave with a solution of 1 litre/1¾ pints/1 qt hot water and 4 tablespoons baking soda. Be sure to wring your cloth or sponge out well before wiping, as you don't want water to get into the workings through any little perforations in the inside of the oven. Tackle stubborn splashes with dry baking soda on a damp cloth or sponge and rinse clean. Dry the inside of the microwave and replace the turntable. You can wipe down the outside using the same solution.

An alternative way of effectively freshening up the microwave is to make a paste using 1 tsp of white vinegar, 50 ml/2 fl oz/¼ cup of baking soda and 6 drops of lemon oil. Simply apply this paste to the inside surfaces of the microwave and then rinse with cold water. If you leave the door of the microwave open for a while then the air will help to dry your clean and bacteria-free microwave.

More Microwave Magic

Another way to freshen your microwave is to add a couple of tablespoons of baking soda to a half-full cup or mug of hot water or use a shallow bowl of equal parts vinegar and water (make sure the cup/mug/bowl is microwave-safe). Put in the microwave on full power and boil for a few minutes. The steam will condense on the inside of the warm oven, loosening splatters of food and leaving it damp. All you need to do is wipe over with kitchen paper, a cloth or sponge, and then dry. Alternatively, placing one or two slices of lemon in a cup of water and running the microwave on high for 30 seconds will achieve the same effect.

If you must leave your microwave door closed when it's not in use you can eliminate musty smells by leaving a small open container of baking soda inside. A ramekin, cup or glass yogurt pot is ideal. Just remember to

remove it before using the oven and replace it afterwards. Stir the contents each time you do and replace the whole lot every two or three months.

Freshen up Your Fridge

Fridges need a complete spring clean every now and again, especially if something has gone off in there and the smell just won't go away. Remove all the food, shelves, drawers and containers, and wipe them over, along with all surfaces and nooks, with a solution of hot water and baking soda on a clean cloth or sponge (an old toothbrush is useful for difficult crannies, and you can use dry powder on the wet brush for stubborn marks). Rinse and dry carefully before switching the appliance back on.

Equal parts of white vinegar and water make an effective and safe cleaner for both the inside and outside of fridges. If you have got mould or mildew lurking in shelves and fridge drawers, zap them with undiluted white vinegar.

And Don't Forget the Freezer

If you have to defrost your freezer, wipe it over inside with a solution of 4 tablespoons baking soda to 1 litre/1¾ pints/1 qt warm water. Wipe over all surfaces and dry before turning the freezer back on.

If your freezer is frost-free it can be tempting to leave it for eons without cleaning it. But even frost-free freezers appreciate a wipe down inside from time to time. Use the same solution as above.

Clean on the Inside, Clean on the Outside

Kitchen appliances, stoves, fridges and so on can get amazingly grimy when you're not looking. Wipe the whole lot over regularly using a solution of baking soda and warm water. Use a cloth or sponge and wring out to avoid drips.

Dishwasher Cleaner

Although you can buy dishwasher fresheners and cleaners, using half a lemon gives just as good a result. Cut the lemon in half and impale it onto one of the upright prongs inside the dishwasher. The acid in the lemon will degrease the appliance and the fresh lemon smell will linger for several cycles.

Once a month, remove soap build-up from dishwashers by pouring 120 ml/4 fl oz/½ cup white vinegar into the bottom of the unit – or placed in a bowl on the top rack. Run the machine on full cycle without dishes or detergent.

Kettle De-scaler

Lime and mineral deposits that have built up in kettles – and in coffee makers – can be shifted by boiling up – or brewing up – enough white vinegar to fill the pot to ¾ full for five minutes. Leave the vinegar in the kettle or coffee maker overnight then rinse out with cold water.

Odor Removal

Fridge (Odor) Magnet

Strong cheese is great, but things like that can leave a not-so-great smell in the fridge. Fight back by leaving an open container of baking soda in there to absorb strong smells and eliminate stale odors. Stir the contents regularly and replace every two or three months or you'll find the baking soda itself is starting to pong!

If you place half a lemon in a small dish at the back of the fridge this can really help as the lemon absorbs the smell for a good length of time. So when you have to put your head into the fridge to clean it, the job won't seem quite so distasteful.

A Fresher Salad Crisper

While you're dealing with the fridge, sprinkle the bottom of the salad drawer with a little dry baking soda, then cover with a layer of paper towel. Wipe out and change about every three months.

And a Fresher Air Freshener

Fill a small bowl almost to the top (choose a pretty one for added effect) with baking soda and add a few drops of your favorite essential oil. Place anywhere in the house that you need to keep things smelling sweet. Add more oil when the effect starts to wane and replace the whole lot about every three months.

When it isn't convenient to have an open bowl around (such as under a sink), cut the feet off a clean old pair of tights and fill the foot with soda. Knot the leg and place this inside the other cut-off foot. Knot this again and put it anywhere you need to eliminate stale smells.

'Vacuum' Your Flask

Get rid of musty or unappetizing smells in a vacuum flask by simply adding
a teaspoonful of baking soda, filling it with hot water, then leaving it
to soak for at least 30 minutes. Empty and rinse well with cold
water. And leave the top off if you're not going to use it
for a while.

Alternatively, clean them out regularly by filling
with warm water and 120 ml/4 fl oz/½ cup
white vinegar and letting them sit for
a couple of hours. Any residue
can be 'scoured' away by
adding a small handful of
uncooked rice. Put the lid
on the flask and shake well,
then rinse and let it air dry.

Onion Odor Eaters

Remove the odor of onion and garlic from wooden or other porous surfaces by sprinkling some baking soda on
to a damp cloth and rubbing it into the surface. Rinse with water, or leave for about half an hour to work for
stronger smells.

Plastic Food Boxes

Plastic can absorb strong smells and less-than-appetizing odors can build up in plastic food boxes, especially
if they are left closed or weren't scrupulously clean when put away. Banish those musty odors by washing the
container in a hot water and baking soda solution, then sprinkle about three tablespoons of soda into the base
of the container and top up with hot water. Put the lid on and shake gently over the sink, then leave for at least
a couple of hours to work. Rinse out and wash again as usual.

Alternatively, wash food containers in a solution of equal parts white vinegar and water, and then rinse clean.
Store with the lids off. If odors persist, place a slice of bread soaked in white vinegar in the food container (lid
on) overnight: the smell should have gone by the next day.

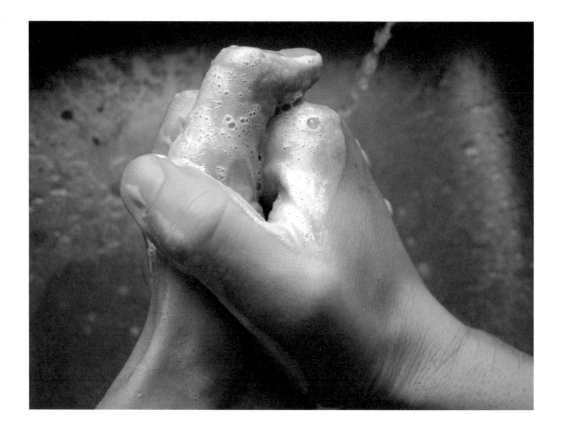

Smelly Hands?

If you've just been chopping onions or garlic, peeling potatoes or handling fish, it can be difficult to erase the smell, even with soap. Baking soda will get rid of the whiff – sprinkle some on to wet hands, rub together well and rinse off.

Seasonal Smells

Musty smells can build up in food containers that are only used during certain times of the year. To prevent this, sprinkle the insides of picnic hampers and cool boxes with a little baking soda before putting away. Wipe out with a damp cloth before using.

Ban Smelly Trash Cans

If your kitchen trash can has a nasty smell that just won't go away, make a solution of 200 g/7 oz/1 cup baking soda in warm water. Pour it into the trash can and top up with more warm water. Leave it to soak for an hour or two, then empty down a drain or the toilet. Make sure you rinse and dry carefully, as bacteria and mould (the cause of bad smells) multiply much faster in warm, steamy conditions.

To prevent smells building up in the first place, sprinkle a little baking soda in the bottom of the trash can, then line the base with a couple of sheets of newspaper, before inserting a (biodegradable) trash can liner.

If a liner leaks, don't ignore it. Deal with it right away by wiping out the trash can with a baking soda solution and rinsing with clean water. Change the newspaper and baking soda regularly, every month or so, to keep things really fresh.

Or, why not try putting some lemon peel in the bottom of your trash can – it really does help rid your kitchen of that trash can smell.

And Bread Box Mould

Accumulated crumbs in the bottom of a bread box can easily turn mouldy (ugh). Make sure you tip them out regularly and wipe over the inside of the box with a solution of baking soda and warm water. Remember to dry the box out thoroughly and allow it to cool before you place fresh bread in it, or the mould will return.

Bathrooms

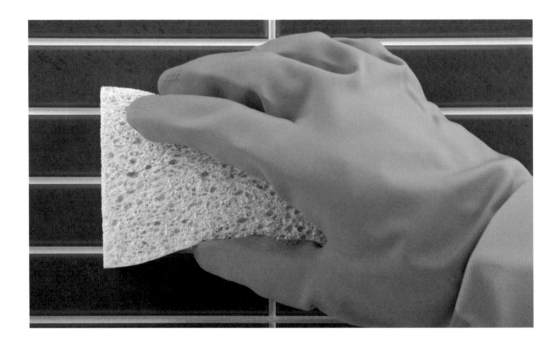

All-over Clean

For general bathroom cleaning, including the bath, basin, shower tray and wall tiles, mix a paste of baking soda and water and use it like cream cleaner on a damp cloth or sponge. And get rid of more stubborn stains with dry baking soda on a damp cloth or sponge. Rinse well to remove any streaks and wipe dry.

Alternatively, use 2 tbsp of lemon juice mixed with 900 ml/1½ pints/3¾ cups of very hot water to help remove scum. Use a spray bottle to coat the layers of soap scum and let the mixture do its job for about 10 minutes before wiping it off with a clean, damp cloth. The acid in the lemon juice cuts through soap scum. The solution works equally well on tiles, shower cubicles, sinks or work surfaces. They will all look shiny and the whole bathroom will smell good. If necessary you can apply neat lemon juice directly onto a sponge or cloth and wash the affected area. Leave the lemon juice to work for a few hours before rinsing it off.

Sweet Smells

Baking soda is perfectly safe for all surfaces, and a couple of drops of essential oil added to the cleaning mix will add extra freshness, so no need for harmful air sprays. Give lemon, pine, tea tree or ylang-ylang a try.

Tap Dancing

If you live in a hard-water area there's a good chance that there's a limescale deposit around the base of your taps – annoying and hard to shift. Not any more – mix some baking soda with a little vinegar and brush the fizzy paste on the offending areas. Leave for about half an hour then rub gently and rinse clean. This works equally well for all hard-water marks in the bathroom, including on glass shower screens.

Bath Time

Baking soda is safe for cleaning all types of baths, but you probably don't always want the bother of cleaning it straight after you've had a soak. No problem: just sprinkle a couple of tablespoons of baking soda into the bathwater before you pull out the plug and your bath will be as clean as you are.

To remove tide marks in your basin or bathtub, try filling with hot water to a level just above the mark and adding a generous amount of white vinegar. Leave it to soak for a couple of hours. Drain away the water and the marks should be much easier to scrub away.

Grimy Nonslip Strips?

Nonslip strips are a useful safety measure but difficult to keep looking spotless. You'll find they get dingy after a while, which may also make them less effective. The answer? Wet the strips and sprinkle with baking soda. Leave to work for about half an hour, then rub clean with a sponge or cloth and rinse well. Job done.

Be Kind to Your Loo

Proprietary toilet cleaners use harsh, caustic chemicals such as bleach, which can stain your clothes if it splashes, harm your hands and, of course, end up in the water supply. Be gentle with your loo: instead, sprinkle some baking soda around the bowl, leave for about half an hour, and then scrub with a toilet brush and flush. Remove more stubborn marks by sprinkling the toilet bowl with baking soda and pouring a dash of white wine vinegar on top. Use a toilet brush to scrub the bowl clean with the bubbling froth that results.

Alternatively, pour about 600 ml/1 pint/2½ cups white vinegar slowly over the sides of the bowl last thing at night. A once-a-week treatment should also help keep away those marks that appear just above the water line in the bowl.

Sitting Comfortably?

Any kind of toilet seat will come up like new when wiped over with a mild solution of baking soda. Don't forget to do the underneath of the seat and lid too. When you've finished, tip the rest of the solution down the toilet for a really thorough clean. If you add a little lemon juice to the soda the solution will also freshen up the whole bathroom.

Flushed with Success

Every few weeks sprinkle some baking soda in your cistern. Leave overnight then flush the next day for a sparkly clean toilet.

Keep Your Drains Running Clear

If not flushed through, soap, shower gel and bath oil residues can build up in the plug hole – more so if there are hairs in there too! Regular drain cleaning helps minimize unpleasant smells and guards against blockages. Use a funnel and pour 4–5 tablespoons baking soda into the plughole. Next, pour in 120 ml/4 fl oz/½ cup white vinegar and watch it foam and fizz. When the fizzing stops, flush through with very hot water. Wait five minutes then flush through with cold water. As well as clearing the blockage, you have also killed and flushed away any odor-creating bacteria that were hiding there.

Shower Power

Any type of shower cubicle can be cleaned quickly and effectively with baking soda-and-water paste. If you're feeling lavish, add a little shampoo or shower gel to the mix for a nice smell.

If you live in a hard-water area you'll know that glass shower doors soon get covered in annoying water marks. Don't worry: just wipe the glass over with a little white vinegar on a cloth or sponge, and then rub over with a sprinkle of baking soda. Rinse well and then squeegee the glass for streak-free spotlessness you can be proud of. Keep a squeegee in the shower and get all the family to have a quick run over the surfaces with it after each shower. It'll cut down on cleaning enormously.

Clear Your Head

Lime scale deposits can quickly clog up the holes in shower heads, so another common problem in hard-water areas is blocked showerheads – not what you need first thing in the morning. If you're able to remove the head, soak it in a mixture made up of 250 ml/8 fl oz/1 cup vinegar with 3 tablespoons baking soda in a suitable container slightly bigger than the head until the limescale has completely dissolved.

If for any reason you can't remove the head to clean it, tip the baking soda-and-vinegar

mixture into a strong plastic bag, a little bigger than the showerhead, and tie or tape it in place over the head so it's in close contact with the frothy solution. Leave in place for the mixture to work its magic for about half an hour, then remove the bag and rinse the head with clean warm water. Run water through the head to clear any residue and you'll soon be singing in the shower again. This works for taps too, but you can also try fixing a plastic cup over the end! Let the tap sit in the mixture for an hour or so, then rinse off with cold water.

Shiny Showers

Soapy watermarks are unsightly on shower cubicles and screens, and if you live in a hard water area, they can be permanently etched into the 'glass' and ruin its clean looks. At the end of your shower, wipe them down with a solution of equal parts water and white vinegar. Finally, remove all traces of water and vinegar with a squeegee, and leave the shower door open to air dry. Tackle sliding shower door tracks by pouring in neat white vinegar to clean and disinfect. Leave it to sit overnight then mop out with a dry sponge. For really gruesome tracks, get scrubbing with a re-cycled toothbrush.

Curtains for Mouldy Shower Curtains

A mouldy shower curtain is the last thing you want flapping around when you're trying to get clean. Soak yours regularly in warm water with about 5 tablespoons baking soda (the bath is a good place for this). Give it a slosh around a few times, then squeeze out and hang to drip dry. Always let shower curtains dry flat after washing, otherwise you'll find the mould will be back again. Not nice.

For mouldy patches or stubborn stains, make up a thick paste of baking soda and rub clean using a sponge, cloth or old nailbrush or toothbrush.

Machine-washable shower curtains can be laundered on the gentle setting with about 100 g/4 oz/½ cup baking soda or half that amount of mild washing powder and the same of baking soda. Throw in a couple of towels to absorb suds and water, and help wash the curtain (which is probably waterproof!) more effectively. Adding 250 ml/8 fl oz/1 cup white vinegar to the rinse cycle will help.

CAUTION: Don't use the spin cycle or you could end up with a permanently creased curtain (and shower curtains aren't usually designed to be ironed). Drip dry instead in an airy place (outside is ideal) or hang it back up in the shower and leave the window open.

Tiles

Soap, shampoo, shower gel and bath foam inevitably get splashed on tiles. Bring dull tiles back to brightness by washing them with a solution of 120 ml/4 fl oz/½ cup white vinegar in 1 litre/2 pints/4 cups warm water.

Grout

Tile grout loses its whiteness and turns gray with age and dirt over time, but its rough surface and porous nature also makes it an ideal home for bacteria to thrive. A re-cycled toothbrush or nailbrush dipped in neat white vinegar will kill germs, and whiten the grout.

Say Goodbye to Bathroom Odors

Musty smells can lurk in bathroom cabinets and cupboards, particularly under basins where there might be slight leakage from pipes and taps. Keep your bathroom storage areas smelling fresh by putting a small, open container of baking soda in each one; this will also help absorb damp.

If you use baking soda as an air freshener in your bathroom, remember to replace it about every three months, but don't throw it in the trash can – tip it down the toilet, leave for a while, then flush, and you'll get extra value from it.

Leaving an open bowl of baking soda outside the bathroom or by the toilet will help to absorb any nasty whiffs. Choose a pretty container that goes with the room scheme and, again, replace the contents about every three months. Add a few drops of essential oil for a luxurious touch.

Banish Musty Bathroom Trash Cans

Bathroom trash cans can quickly get a bit musty, which is both unhygienic and unpleasant. If your can is washable, rinse it clean with a solution of baking soda and dry carefully. All trash cans, whether washable or not, will definitely benefit from a sprinkle of soda in the bottom, covered with a square of paper towel. Tip or wipe out the powder about every three months and replace the paper as necessary.

Laundry

You can see them all as you walk around the store – stain removers, clothes' whiteners, special washing powder or gel tabs for colored clothes, fabric softeners. Is it not ironic that although all of these might work, baking soda, lemons and vinegar are equally effective for the majority of laundry jobs? Lemon juice, for example, can remove the most stubborn stains, including rust and mildew, because of its amazing bleaching properties. The bonus is that you get sweet-smelling clothes and save money on expensive products.

Stain & Odor Removal

Painless Stain Removal

Any type of stain is always best dealt with before it has time to dry because once the mark starts to set it will become much more difficult to remove. Because of its unique formulation, baking soda is great for many types of stain removal as well as for general laundry.

CAUTION: Some fabrics that are optimistically described as machine or hand washable are really not suitable for this kind of washing at all. To be on the safe side, always test stain removal techniques on an inconspicuous area of the material first, especially if it's your absolute favorite item of clothing.

Blood Simple

Bloodstains are always difficult to remove, as anyone who watches crime TV shows will tell you. Baking soda, however, will normally remove blood from washable clothing. For small areas of blood, dampen the stain with cold water, but not hot water as this sets blood stains, making them far more difficult to remove. Rub baking soda into the stained area with an old toothbrush or clean nailbrush. Leave the baking soda paste on to soak for a while and repeat the process if necessary. Launder as normal.

If you can get to the bloodstain quickly, you can also try pouring undiluted white vinegar directly onto the spot and letting it soak in for 5–10 minutes before blotting with a clean cloth. Repeat if necessary and then launder as usual. Older, set-in stains can be successfully removed by treating the affected area with a solution of 3 tablespoons white vinegar, 2 tablespoons liquid detergent and 1 litre/2 pints/4½ cups warm water. Repeatedly sponge and blot the stained area and then launder.

Blood Not So Simple

For larger areas of blood, add 200 g/7 oz/1 cup baking soda and 250 ml/8 fl oz/1 cup white vinegar to a bucket of cold water. Swirl the mixture around well and then add the bloodstained clothing. Leave for several hours – overnight is ideal – then launder as usual.

Vomit and Urine

There's no nice way to say this, but vomit and urine are acidic. The first thing to do is thoroughly rinse any stains under a cold tap as soon as possible after the event to avoid lasting damage to the fabric. Sprinkle the area with baking soda and leave for about half an hour before washing. Baking soda will neutralize the acid and prevent it from permanently damaging clothing.

For larger areas of vomit, scrape off as much as you can, then soak the item or items in a bucket of cool water to which you have added 200 g/7 oz/1 cup baking soda.

Couldn't Face Cleaning It at the Time?

If acidic stains or spills have dried onto clothes, don't soak them in water as the acid will be reactivated and will start to harm the clothes. This explains why clothes that have had acid splashed on them go into the wash intact and come out with holes. Instead, mix some baking soda with a little water and spread on to the stain. This will neutralize the acid before it has time to start eating into the fabric. Leave the baking soda on for an hour or two, then wash as normal.

This also works for other acid spills such as lemon, orange and other citrus juices (which, although they're good for you, are acidic), acidic toilet cleaners and battery acid. You can also try this for wine spills and other fruit stains.

No Sweat!

Scrub those unpleasant perspiration stains from washable clothing with a nailbrush and a paste of baking soda and water, leave for at least an hour to work effectively, longer for bad stains, then wash as normal. Not only will this remove the stain, it'll get rid of the smell too. Phew ...

Rusty Clothing?

Rust isn't just a problem for suits of armor. Rust stains can also appear on suits made of cloth and other clothing. Soak the area with lemon juice, then sprinkle generously with baking soda. Leave overnight to work, then rinse off and wash as normal.

Or try lemons. Whatever you do, don't be tempted to put proprietary bleach onto a rust stain because all it will do is set hard. Instead, sprinkle the clothing with a generous amount of table salt. Squeeze a lemon over the salt and place the item of clothing outside in the sun. If possible keep it in direct sunlight for several hours, adding more lemon juice if the clothing begins to dry out. Before you pop it into the washing machine, with added lemon juice of course, brush the salt off what should now be a faded stain.

Ease off Grease

Grease stains can be so frustrating. They just seem to come back wash after wash. Don't despair: sprinkle fresh grease splashes with baking soda and leave for an hour or two to work. Then drip a little water on to the powder and scrub gently. Rinse off and wash as normal.

For dry-clean only clothes, just sprinkle the dry powder on as above, leave to work and brush off with a clean, soft brush.

Gray-collar Worker?

Greasy, discolored shirt collars and grimy cuffs will get short shrift if you scrub them with a paste of baking soda and water and a nailbrush. Leave the mixture to soak for half an hour or so, then wash as normal.

For severe stains, try drizzling a little white vinegar on to the soaking mixture. The resulting froth will deliver the extra grease-busting power that you need.

Persuade Suede to Come Clean

Suede is all too easy to stain and expensive to dry-clean. Before you head to the cleaners, try gently rubbing dry baking soda into stains on suede, using a soft brush. Leave it to set, then brush off carefully.

Grease spots on suede garments, shoes and handbags can be removed if you dip a clean toothbrush into neat white vinegar and very gently brush the spot. Do not scrub or you will damage the nap. Let the spot air dry then brush with a suede brush and repeat if required. Suede items can be revived generally by a gentle wipe over with a sponge dipped in white vinegar.

CAUTION: Don't forget to try on an inconspicuous part of the garment before you proceed to ensure it doesn't have any adverse effects.

Ballpoint Blobs?

The primary carrier for the color in ball-point and roller-ball pen inks is a very fine oil – often castor oil – so ink marks can be treated with white vinegar, which cuts through the grease and lets the color flow off the affected fabric. Treat the ink stain first by blotting with undiluted white vinegar, and then gently rub in a paste of 2 parts white vinegar and 3 parts cornstarch. Let the paste dry completely on the ink stain and then launder as usual.

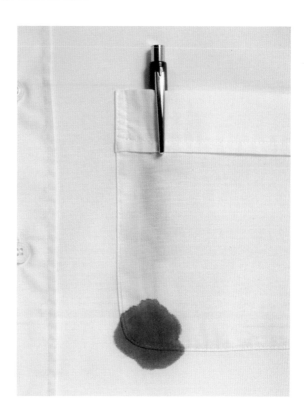

Alternatively, for white clothing, try sprinkling table salt onto the stain and generously apply neat lemon juice on top. Put the item of clothing in direct sunlight for as long as possible, moistening regularly with more lemon juice. Wash as normal, but if the stain has only lightened and not disappeared then repeat the whole process.

Ink Stains on Leather

Ballpoint pen or other types of ink can be removed from leather clothing but you need to act fast. Sprinkle a little baking soda on the stain, leave for a couple of hours to absorb the ink, then brush off and buff up the leather.

New Baby, New Clothes

New baby clothes often contain a dressing that stiffens the fabric so it looks good in the shop. Perversely this can cause soreness and rashes on delicate baby skin. Rinse this unnecessary chemical concoction out of the clothing before the bambino wears it by washing the offending garment in warm water and a little mild detergent to which you have added 100 g/4 oz/½ cup baking soda.

Some adults also find their skin is irritated by these fabric dressings, so just follow the same instructions.

Diapers

Disposable diapers can leave a dubious ecological legacy. If you are using the traditional toweling alternative, soak the dirty diapers in baking soda and water overnight. This not only curbs unpleasant smells, but means that you can use less detergent in the machine when it comes to washing them.

Reduce Rashes

If, in common with many people, you're allergic to commercial washing powders and find they irritate your skin, try using 200 g/7 oz/1 cup baking soda in your wash instead. This is also ideal for getting baby clothes lovely and soft.

In the Swim

Remove damaging chlorine or salt from your bathing costume after a trip to the pool or swimming in the sea by soaking the garment for an hour or two in warm water to which you have added a handful of baking soda. Wash as usual and your swimwear will keep looking good for much longer, and it won't have that worryingly bleachy smell when you next put it on.

Tune up Your Washing Machine

Adding half a cup of baking soda to a load of washing will improve the performance of your usual liquid detergent, helping with the removal of stains and grease. And, as baking soda acts as a very effective water softener, you'll find you will get the same results with considerably less detergent than usual.

What's more, your white clothes will come out looking whiter, and brightly colored clothes will keep their color longer. All for a few pennies.

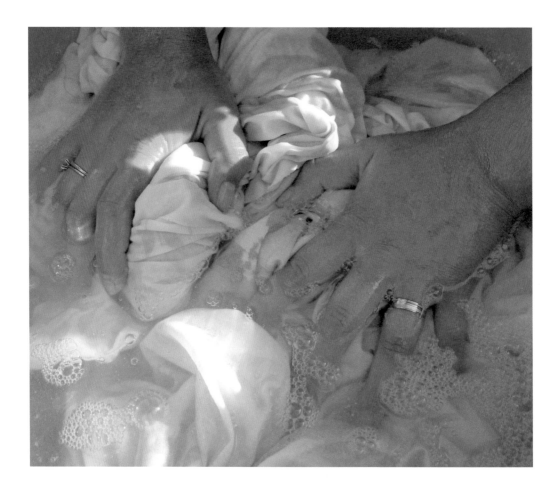

A Handy Hand-washing Tip

You can hand wash delicate articles in warm water with 50 g/2 oz/¼ cup baking soda and about a tablespoon of hand-washing laundry liquid. Wash and rinse as usual, adding a tablespoon of baking soda to the final rinse as a softener.

CAUTION: Before you wash anything delicate you should pay particular attention to the washing instructions that came with the garment.

A Soul Mate for Your Sole-plate

The sole-plate of your iron can easily get marked and hard water will soon block up the steam holes. Remedy this by unplugging the iron and leaving it to cool, then rub over the plate with baking soda and water paste on a sponge or cloth. Wipe over with a clean damp cloth and buff dry.

Smoke Gets in Your Clothes

To remove smoke smells from clothes, whether from cigarettes or bonfires, add half a cup of baking soda at the rinse cycle. This will also get rid of the smell of mothballs or musty cupboards that might be lingering on your clothes.

Alternatively, soak smoky clothes in a solution of baking soda before you put them in the washing machine. This works well for clothes tainted with smoke, or clothes that haven't been dried properly and have developed that horribly rancid 'old dishcloth' smell.

Mildew Patches

If there are areas of mildew on clothing that's been in storage, rub with a paste of baking soda and water before washing.

Alternatively, try a trusty lemon. Sprinkle the stains generously with table salt and liberally pour lemon juice over the salt. Then let that magic combination of lemon and sun remove the stain. Leave it to dry in direct sunlight for several hours, but continue to keep the area moist by adding more lemon juice periodically. Brush off the salt before putting the item in the washing machine – and don't forget you can add more lemon juice to the wash cycle too if needed. The lemon juice will also help eliminate the smell of mildew, which can so often linger, even after washing.

CAUTION: Lemon juice can have a bleaching effect, so is safest used only on light colors.

Perspiration Inspiration

Baking soda not only deals with sweat stains but banishes the smell too. This can be a real boon as work clothes and sports garb can still retain that acrid smell (sorry, there's no nicer way to describe it) even after normal laundering. Soak offending items overnight in a solution of 100 g/4 oz/½ cup baking soda and 4 litres/7 pints/4 qts warm water before laundering as usual.

Alternatively, mix together a potion of half lemon juice and half water, then scrub gently at the stain to remove any ugly marks.

Deodorant Stains

Antiperspirants and deodorants can leave horrible white marks on clothes. These can be

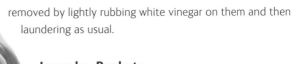

removed by lightly rubbing white vinegar on them and then laundering as usual.

Laundry Baskets

Banish the whiff of fusty laundry baskets by sprinkling baking soda over the dirty washing. This also prevents the basket itself from becoming smelly. Add a further handful of baking soda each time you put another load of grubby clothing in.

Feeling Creative?

Popping a homemade sachet into your laundry basket will absorb unpleasant smells for months. Simply cut out a circle of lightweight fabric, about the size of a dinner plate, and place a large handful of baking soda in the center. Add some lavender or a few drops of your favorite essential oil. Gather the fabric up around the powder and secure with an elastic band. Tie a ribbon around the band to hang against the side of the basket or drop it into the bottom. Nice.

Freshen White Laundry

Some washing powders claim they wash whiter, and that it shows, but they've probably not used lemons. The bleaching effect of lemon juice can really work on keeping your whites white. Add lemon juice to your normal wash cycle. How much you pop into the washing machine will depend on the amount of white laundry you are hoping to whiten. For a complete bed set of whites use the juice of one or two lemons, but for a couple of white tops just squeeze in half a lemon.

To Bleach or Whiten

Rather than risking the use of proprietary bleaching products to remove stains, why not try using lemons instead? The problem with using bleach is that it can actually stain clothes itself. This is because it can lift elements of iron from the water system and stain your clothing during the wash cycle.

For a failsafe way of removing stains or whitening clothes, soak them in a mixture of half lemon juice and half water before washing. If the clothes are badly stained you might find it useful, in addition to the pre-soak, to add lemon juice to the washing machine too. Those stains definitely will not survive both these treatments!

Don't forget the power of the sun and lemon combined. Your whites, once pre-soaked and then washed with the added lemon juice, will dazzle if you hang them on the line on a sunny day. The sun will help bleach those stains, too!

Alternatively, white garments or fabrics that have yellowed can be returned to their former glory by soaking them overnight in a solution of 12 parts warm water and 1 part white vinegar and then laundered the following day as usual.

If you habitually add bleach to the detergent in your washing machine, also add 50 g/2 oz/¼ cup baking soda if you are using a front-loading machine, or twice as much for top-loaders. Your usual bleach will not only work harder but you will only need to use half the quantity that you normally do. Your white wash will come up brighter, and baking soda is much kinder to your clothes. It's gentle on colored items too.

White Sports Socks

To keep those white sports socks white and eliminate the discoloration you so often get on the bottoms of the feet, try boiling them in a pan of equal amounts of hot water and lemon juice. Works on dingy washcloths too.

Alternatively, they can be made brighter and given an antibacterial treatment by placing about 1.7 litres/3 pints/7¼ cups cold water and about 145 ml/5 fl oz/⅔ cup white vinegar into a large saucepan and bringing it to a boil. Put the dingy socks – or washcloths – into a bucket and pour the boiling vinegar solution over them. Let them soak overnight and the next day, launder them as usual.

Keep Clothes Bright

There are a number of tips available for keeping your colored clothes bright and to prevent them from fading, including washing inside out and hanging out to dry inside out. Another useful tip for those who like to use nature's way is to add 120 ml/4 fl oz/½ cup of white vinegar to the washing machine. Vinegar doesn't smell

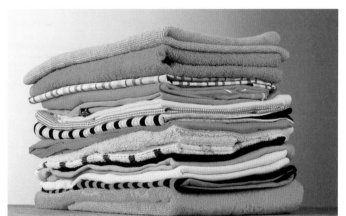

good, even though it is effective for retaining the vibrancy of color, so add a few drops of lemon juice to the vinegar before putting it into the washing machine and this really improves the smell.

CAUTION: Do not add too much lemon juice because of its bleaching properties.

Whiten Athletic Shoes

If your tennis or canvas athletic shoes have begun to look a bit grubby, there's no need to reach for the bleach bottle to whiten them. Lemon juice will do it. Spray them with lemon juice all over – inside and out. Then place them in the direct sunlight to dry. They will be stain-free and much whiter when you return to them and they'll probably smell much better too!

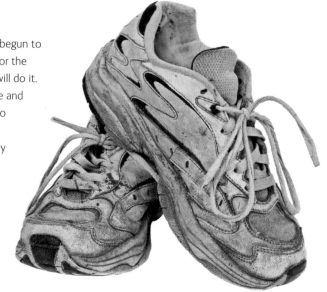

Tea-stain Removal

Before you decide to dispose of that favorite top or other item you have spilled tea over, have a go at removing the stain with lemon. As with all stains on clothing, it is wise to treat it as soon as possible for an effective removal.

If your clothing can be washed in hot water, try pouring 250 ml/8 fl oz/1 cup of lemon juice into the washing machine and wash the item straight away. If this is not possible, at the very least sprinkle some lemon juice over the tea stain. This will remove the color from the stain. Then wash it in the machine, including the lemon juice of course, at the earliest opportunity.

Fruit and Fruit Juice Stain Removal

We already know that lemon juice is effective for removing berry stains from hands and kitchen work surfaces. Well, it is just as effective on removing fruit stains from clothing. It doesn't really matter what variety of fruit has found its way onto your clothes, because lemon juice works well on them all. If you sprinkle some neat lemon juice over the stain before washing it will help the stain to fade. Add more lemon juice to the washing machine and it will never survive!

Scorch-mark Removal

It has happened to all of us; you're busy ironing and someone rings the doorbell or telephones and you leave the iron face down on the clothing. When you return there is a brownish, iron-shaped mark that you feel sure will never come out in the wash. If it happens again, try lemon juice. Squeeze a lemon over the stain and let it dry in direct sunlight. Timing will depend on the thickness of the fabric and the intensity of the sun. Hopefully if it hasn't actually burned the fabric, the lemon juice and sunlight combined will lighten the stain, although you may have to repeat the process to make it disappear altogether.

Pre-Wash Stain Removal

White vinegar is such a useful pre-wash stain remover it is worthwhile keeping a spray bottle with a half-and-half solution of white vinegar and water close to hand. As you check over garments before putting them in the washer, treat any heavy grime or underarm perspiration stains with a quick spray of vinegar.

Wine Stains

Wine stains can be removed from cotton and cotton polyester fabrics – but only if you get to the stain within 24 hours! Here you do need to use undiluted white vinegar: sponge it gently on to the stained area and blot with a clean cloth. Repeat until as much of the wine stain as possible has been removed and then wash according to the care label instructions for the garment.

Vintage Lace Restored

Old and antique lace is often very delicate so start any cleaning process by soaking it first in cold water and letting it dry naturally.

If it is still on the yellow side when dry, use a very mild solution of white vinegar and water: 24 parts water and 1 part white vinegar for an overnight soak. Rinse well and allow the lace to dry naturally – in the sun if possible, as this will also help in the 'bleaching' process.

Banish Smells From Suits

A night out can leave your clothes smelling of stale cigarette smoke or even the smell of the food you ate in the restaurant. You can, however, often remove the odor from clothes without resorting to dry cleaning. Put 145 ml/5 fl oz/⅔ cup white vinegar in the bathtub and fill the tub with hot water. Hang the offending garments in your bathroom and close the door and let the 'vinegar steam' impregnate and deodorize the garments for a couple of hours. Afterwards, hang the garments in an open space – not the wardrobe – to let them 'dry out'.

Second-hand Smells

Scouring vintage and second-hand clothing stores can yield fashionable finds, but even though the garments may have been cleaned, they can often have lingering odors. Add 120 ml/4 fl oz/½ cup white vinegar to the wash cycle – or to a bathtub of water if the garment is vintage and needs delicate hand washing. This will deodorize the garment, and kill off any bacteria that may be present.

Clean Machine

You will not get clean clothes from a dirty washing machine, so once in a while, pour in about 230 ml/8 fl oz/1 cup white vinegar and run the washer on a full cycle but without clothes or detergents. This will clean out residual soap scum, remove mineral deposits and deodorize your washing machine.

Kill Bacteria

Because of the acetic acid content, white vinegar has bactericidal properties and so about 120 ml/4 fl oz/½ cup white vinegar added to your washer's rinse cycle will kill off any bacteria present in the wash load, especially if it contains terry diapers (or sweaty sports socks). White vinegar will naturally break down uric acid from baby and children's clothes.

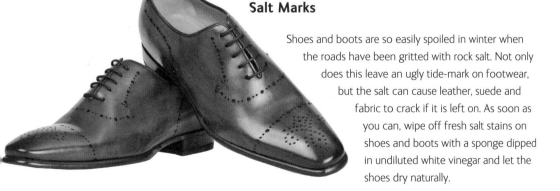

Salt Marks

Shoes and boots are so easily spoiled in winter when the roads have been gritted with rock salt. Not only does this leave an ugly tide-mark on footwear, but the salt can cause leather, suede and fabric to crack if it is left on. As soon as you can, wipe off fresh salt stains on shoes and boots with a sponge dipped in undiluted white vinegar and let the shoes dry naturally.

Condition

Soften It Up

Unless you happen to like your laundry smelling of synthetic perfumes, there is no need for expensive fabric softening liquids or sheets (the latter are also partly responsible for 'furring up' the heating elements of washing machines causing them to overheat and break down!). Baking soda not only washes clothes, it also works well as a fabric softener. Its gentle action is ideal if you find commercial fabric conditioners irritate your skin, or you want to avoid all that plastic packaging. Try adding 100 g/4 oz/½ cup baking soda at the rinse stage or mix with a little warm water and pour into the conditioner drawer of your washing machine. It leaves clothes smelling fresh, but without the artificial, perfumed smell of shop-bought softeners. Baking soda as a softener is particularly good for keeping towels fluffy and soft.

Alternatively, mix two parts water, one part baking soda and one part white vinegar. It will fizz up like mad, but once it has calmed down completely you can pour in into a plastic bottle for storage. Be sure to label it clearly and keep it out of the reach of children. Add about 50 ml/2 fl oz/¼ cup of the mixture to the fabric softener drawer in your machine per wash.

Lint Removal

Some people say that vinegar works well on a piece of cloth or a sponge to remove lint build-up on clothing. And lemon juice works just as well. Soak the cloth or sponge in the lemon juice or vinegar and dab away at the lint. The lemon juice will soak it up. Another way of using a lemon to remove the lint is to treat half a lemon like a piece of sticky tape. The fibrous pulp and pith of the lemon will grab the lint from the clothing as you dab away.

Blanket Reviver

Cotton and wool blankets and bedding can be revived and made soft and fluffy – and free of soap residues and odors – by adding about 230 ml/8 fl oz/1 cup white vinegar to the final rinse cycle.

Banish wrinkles

Sometimes clothes have wrinkles and creases that have dried in: this can happen even when they are brand new from the store. Rather than iron them out, de-wrinkle them by hanging the garment on a clothes hanger and lightly spraying a mist of a solution of 1 part white vinegar and 3 parts water. Let the garment air dry.

Keep Woolens in Shape

If a sweater has emerged from the wash and appears to have grown by yards, do not despair. Make a solution of 1 part white vinegar to 2 parts warm – not hot – water and soak for 20–25 minutes. Gently squeeze out the excess, but do not wring the garment as you will only twist the yarn and stretch it further. When you have squeezed as much water out as you can, lay out the sweater flat on a large folded-up towel and gently arrange the sweater back into shape. Put another towel on top and gently blot the sweater, letting the towels absorb more moisture. Put the sweater flat on a new, dry towel and let it dry naturally.

Shiny Seats

The seats of skirts and trousers can become shiny, even after a single wear. Dip an old, but clean, toothbrush into a solution of equal parts white vinegar and water and gently brush the shiny area. Blot the moisture with a clean towel and let the garment air dry.

Keep Colors Fast

New and old colored garments can loose much of their color in the wash and you can end up with faded or streaky patches. To fix the color, soak colored fabrics and garments for a few minutes in a bowl of diluted white vinegar before you wash them.

Stop Red Running

Red is a notorious color for running in the wash and turning everything washed with it pink: but pre-soaking a new red item in undiluted vinegar before the first wash can limit the amount of red dye that is shed. It is still a good idea to wash dark and colored items separately from white items, but you will find the red items do not loose as much of their color in the long run.

Stay Sharp

Some garments demand razor-sharp creases so use a spray diffuser with a solution of equal parts white vinegar and water and lightly spray the garment before ironing. For some reason, the creases are even sharper if you place a piece of brown paper on the garment and iron onto this rather than directly onto the fabric. Try it for yourself!

Home & Garden

General Household & Home Improvement

Probably the most fundamental reason for using these wonder ingredients around the home is the cost. They are so cheap that needing large quantities to complete a job is not a problem. In addition, because they are natural products, the fact that you may be using large amounts outside does not pose a threat to the environment. To top it off, the refreshing and invigorating smell of lemons symbolizes for many a clean and well-kept home.

Maintenance & DIY

Pliable Plaster

To keep plaster 'wet' for a little longer while you work it smooth on walls, add 2 tablespoons white vinegar to the plaster mix. This will slow down the hardening process and give you a little more time to achieve the perfect, smooth finish.

Strip-ease

Stripping off old wallpaper is a messy job and can be expensive if you have to hire or buy a steam stripper. Before you spend your money, try spraying the wallpaper until it is well saturated with a solution of equal parts water and white vinegar, then scrape away.

If there are tough areas, try scoring the wallpaper with a sharp blade before soaking. Shifting as much wallpaper as possible this way means you are less likely to fill up your home with condensation.

Sticky Fingerprints

The acid in vinegar cuts through grease so it is a good cleaner for surfaces (like staircase walls where sticky hands have made a trail) prior to painting, especially if you are using a water-based emulsion: paint over oily or greasy marks and they will 'float' to the surface of your new paint, just like an oil and vinegar salad dressing that has 'separated'.

Restore Paintbrushes

OK, so you had enough of painting the room and you needed a break, but you left the paintbrush overnight and it's now hardened so much that you can't use it. Do not discard just yet! Instead, soak synthetic bristle brushes that have dried-on paint in undiluted white vinegar until the paint dissolves. Brush handles usually

have a hole in them: thread a skewer or long nail though the hole and balance the brush on the edge of jar, so the bristles are suspended in the vinegar and that way you will not get bent bristles.

Bring Brushes Back from the Dead!

If the above vinegar remedy still leaves your paintbrushes looking beyond all hope, before you consign them to the DIY graveyard try this: bring 115–230 ml/4–8 fl oz/½–1 cup white vinegar or lemon juice to a boil in an old saucepan and immerse the bristles in the boiling solution for 10–15 minutes. Then wash with warm soapy water and rinse clean. You'll have bendy bristles again.

Remove Paint Fumes

Even today's water-based and 'green' paints still have a paint odor: always make sure that when you decorate, the room is well ventilated. At the end of the job you can get rid of lingering paint smells by placing a couple of shallow bowls of neat white vinegar in the newly decorated room.

Squeaky Clean

Mildew and dust can be a problem in older properties and during renovation. Wiping the walls with undiluted white vinegar will 'kill' mildew and dampen down the dust making removal easier. For hard to reach ceilings, try using a sponge mop on a pole!

Rusty Saws and Bolts

Rusted saws and the blades of cutting tools can be 'sharpened' by immersing the metal in undiluted white vinegar for a couple of days. Loosen up corroded nuts and bolts in the same way, and paint vinegar onto rusted screws and hinges before you try to undo them.

Wonderful Wood

Stripped wood in all its natural beauty looks wonderful but can become dull with dirt. Taking off the dirt does not mean you have to take off a layer of wood as well – as you would with an electric sander or stripper.

Before you go down the electric route, try a simpler (and less noisy) solution: mix 600 ml/1 pint/2½ cups of warm water with 4 tablespoons white vinegar – or even cider vinegar – and 2 tablespoons olive oil in a sealable

bottle or jar. Give it a shake and then apply to the wood with a clean cloth. Let the 'dressing' soak into the wood for a few minutes and then buff to a shine with a dry cloth.

Remove Scratches on Furniture

You can remove minor scratches on furniture by mixing together equal parts of lemon juice and vegetable oil or olive oil. Rub the mixture onto the affected area quite thoroughly with a soft, dry cloth, then give it a good buff up with another clean cloth. This is also a good recipe for making your own wooden furniture polish. The olive oil leaves a really impressive shine, with the bonus of the clean smell of lemons.

Painting Cement

Light gray cement may not be your favorite finish, so enliven it with color. Painted cement, however, does have a tendency to peel after a while, but by painting the cement first with an initial coat of white vinegar and letting it dry, you will find that the paint adheres for much longer. You can also use this technique for painting galvanized metal.

Avoid Concrete and Cement Burns

We often think that only heat and acid cause burns, but strong alkalis can also cause skin blistering. It is the lime in concrete and cement mix that is highly alkaline and contact with the skin should be avoided as it can cause skin cracking and even eczema. Wash dried concrete and cement off your skin with undiluted white vinegar to neutralize the lime, then wash in warm soapy water.

Bright Bricks

Attractive brickwork, whether on floors, walls or fireplaces can often be marred by white or green salt 'tide marks' called efflorescence. This occurs when the mortar or masonry units dry out and the soluble alkaline salts migrate to the surface. Washing away with water can work for a while, but more often than not it brings more salt to the surface. To stop the problem recurring try washing brickwork with an acid solution to neutralize the alkaline salts: 230 ml/8 fl oz/1 cup white vinegar in a bucket of warm water may just do the trick.

Outdoors

Preserve those Tools

Shovels, spades, garden forks, rakes and trowels, and indeed all your garden tools should be put away for the winter in a clean state to help preserve them. To help do this you can make a thick paste with baking soda and white vinegar to give them a good clean. The paste will also stop rust forming over the winter months.

Polished Pots

If your garden pots are not frost-resistant then they should also be stored away before winter sets in. But if you put them away dirty you will find yourself faced with twice the job of cleaning them in the spring. Use the baking soda and white vinegar paste to clean them and then wash this off with some hot, soapy water. They'll sparkle in the spring!

Potato Trick

If any of your garden tools have been neglected and become rusty you can use a potato and some baking soda to renew them. Just peel the potato and keep dipping it in the baking soda and rub until the rust has all been removed from the metal tool. Shiny again!

Wash that Plastic

Garden furniture is not cheap, so if you want to prolong its life you have to take care of it. Plastic garden furniture should be washed before it is put into storage for the winter. Add 100 g/7 oz/1 cup baking soda to some hot soapy water and wash the furniture with the mix. This will help remove stains too.

Bright Whites

If your garden furniture is all white in color you can keep it that way by adding some lemon juice to your baking soda mix. Squeeze the lemon juice into your hot water and baking soda mix. It is as good as bleaching the white furniture.

Clean the Grill

Cleaning the grill can be a tiresome job and quite a messy one. But to clean the appliance without causing any scratching to the stainless steel surface, try sprinkling some baking soda straight on to a damp brush. Coat the grill well with the baking soda, give it a good scrub then rinse clean.

Pool Perfection

While you're busy cleaning the garden in general, the children's inflatable pool might benefit from a bit of tender loving care too. Get rid of any mold or mildew by rubbing it inside and out with a mix of water, baking soda and white vinegar. Good as new and safe for the children next year.

Birdbaths

Even the birdbath needs a good clean from time to time, but don't worry about harming the creatures that drink from it or bathe in it. Using baking soda and water mixed to a paste will remove all stubborn grime and won't affect the birds at all.

Cleaning Paving, Patios and Decking

Although it might take a whole box of baking soda to clean your paving and patio areas, it is still effective and inexpensive. Wet the baking soda a little bit after you've sprinkled it over your concrete areas and then scrub with a stiff garden broom to remove stains and moss from the concrete.

You could use the sprinkling and brushing technique for cleaning your wooden decking too. Sprinkle the baking soda on and brush with a dry broom, but wash away the dirt and grime with water afterwards.

Mildew on Furniture and Decks

Wooden garden furniture and decking are very attractive additions in any outside space, but they do need regular maintenance. In warm, damp conditions mildew can be a problem so have a handy spray bottle of full strength white vinegar to hand. The mildew will wipe off quite easily and the vinegar will keep it from coming back for a while. For large areas such as decking, use a brush and a bucket.

Shining Shades

Fabric patio umbrellas and awnings are also prone to mildew, especially if they have been stored closed through the winter. These can be cleaned and deodorized using a mix of 230 ml/8 fl oz/1 cup white vinegar, 2 tablespoons dishwashing liquid and a bucket of hot water. Put your gloves on and scrub. Rinse off with clean water and open the umbrella or awning to let it air dry – preferably in the sunshine!

Hygienic Hammocks

Garden hammocks can be wiped down with a baking soda and water mix. This will get rid of any built-up grime and also bring out their color, not to mention making them smell really fresh for you too when you swing next summer.

Cleaner and Safer Toys

Children's garden toys, such as trampolines or slides and seesaws, as well as plastic cars and scooters, all need the baking soda touch. Baking soda mixed with water will bring the colors back to life and keep the dust levels at a minimum. Must be better and healthier for the children to use clean toys in the garden?

Plastic garden toys can become brittle if they are stored away in a warm environment during the winter months. To counteract this effect you can wipe the toys with a mixture of baking soda and white vinegar. The two ingredients when mixed together will clean and protect the toys at the same time.

Secure Repairs

Do you have any repairs that need doing on your garden furniture? If the furniture is plastic and you intend to use superglue, you can make the repair even stronger by adding a little baking soda to the glue. Sprinkle the baking soda on to the superglue while it is still wet.

Snow and Ice

Baking soda acts very much like salt on snow and ice. Because the baking soda, like salt, freezes at a lower temperature than water, it is an ideal way to melt snow once it has lain on your concrete. Sprinkle it over freshly fallen snow to help it melt quickly. Then add some more in case the slush freezes.

For a more preventative measure, if snow and ice are forecast you can stop the water from freezing overnight by sprinkling baking soda on to your concrete. Use it on your pathways and steps in the garden to stop falls and accidents. Sprinkle it generously and cover as much of the concrete as you can.

Vehicles

Oil and Petrol Spills

If you've got a car that leaks oil or petrol on the floor of your garage then you might like to try the baking soda remedy for removing the stain. You just need to sprinkle a mixture of baking soda and salt over the spill. Leave it for a while to soak up all the oil or petrol. Then all you need to do is sweep the floor.

Even if the oil or petrol leaks on to your driveway, baking soda and salt will still lift the stain efficiently. Give the mix plenty of time to soak all the liquid up before you sweep the drive, though.

Odor Removal

If the car has not been used for some time, it can begin to smell musty inside. Neutralize these smells by sprinkling baking soda all-over. You can put it in the trunk, on the seat and on the mats without any fear of damaging the interior upholstery.

Got smelly ashtrays in your car? You can get rid of that lingering smell by putting 120 ml/4 fl oz/½ cup baking soda into the ashtray when it is clean. The baking soda will neutralize the smell of the smoke and leave the whole car deodorized and smelling fresher.

Alternatively, deodorize car mats and remove salt deposits with a solution of equal parts white vinegar and water and sponge it on. Leave it to sink in for a few minutes then blot up with sheets of newspaper or paper towels and let them air dry. You can also spruce up the seat upholstery in the same way, but you will need to do this on a warm day, and leave the windows wide open so it can dry out completely.

Extinguishing Fires

Small fires can be extinguished in a garage or workshop using baking soda. Pour a complete box of the baking soda on to the fire and it will extinguish it. Good idea to keep some on the shelf just in case, particularly if you regularly use a naked flame in the garage or workshop.

You could also keep some baking soda in the trunk of your car. It is particularly effective at extinguishing electrical fires. The baking soda smothers the fire and brings its temperature down quite quickly.

Rusty Bikes

Bicycles can go rusty quite quickly, particularly if they are housed in a garage or shed. Vinegar and baking soda mixed to a paste will give them a general clean, but if there are any rust patches developing, give them a particularly good scrub. The mix should remove the rust quite easily.

Soda Shine

To give the chrome on a bicycle or motorbike an extra shine, apply a baking soda and water paste. Smear it on to the chrome and then leave it to dry naturally in the air. When it is dry you can buff the chrome with a soft cloth and you'll be able to see your face in it.

Bugs on Bikes

To remove bugs that may have got stuck to the wing mirrors of your bicycle or motorbike you can wash them with a mixture of baking soda and water. The bugs will come off quite easily, but you won't scratch the mirror.

On the Road

If your windscreen gets more blurred when it rains and you have turned the wipers on, then your wiper blades are dirty. Clean them off by running a cloth soaked in white vinegar along the entire length of each blade.

Organic De-Icer

Most drivers keep a noxious can of aerosol, chemical de-icer in the car in winter and probably throw it away come spring. Save your money, and a space in the landfill site, by spraying your car windows with a solution of 3 parts white vinegar and 1 part water. You will find that it can keep frost from forming on your windows for up to two weeks.

Lemon Freshness

Air Freshener

To refresh the air in the kitchen, particularly if you've been cooking fish or strong-smelling foods like garlic, cut a lemon in half and immerse it in a pan of water. Bring the water to boil and the aroma will fill the kitchen. It can simmer away for a number of hours, but you may need to top up the water level every now and again.

For extra special occasions, why not add some cloves, cinnamon sticks and a few pieces of orange and apple peel to the lemon and water while it is simmering in your kitchen. It not only smells delightful, but the vapor spreads around the house and it also humidifies the room.

Spray Freshener

You can make your own spray air-freshener by putting equal amounts of water and lemon juice into a spray bottle. It lasts for ages and is so quick and convenient, plus it smells much more natural than the proprietary air-fresheners. For a more intense freshener you could try adding lemon oil instead of fresh lemon juice.

Lemon Oil

Lemon oil can also be good for the mind, levels of concentration and the general feeling of well-being. Try adding a few drops of this essential oil to the water at the top of a ceramic burner as an alternative way to freshen the air in your home. Good for anyone who is having to studying for exams!

Freshen With Light!

Another way of refreshing a room is to put some lemon juice onto a piece of kitchen paper. Then coat your light bulbs with the lemon juice. When the light is turned on the heat from the bulb warms the lemon juice and provides the aroma.

CAUTION: Only apply the lemon juice to light bulbs when they are cold.

Get Rid of Mothball Smells

If it's too late and you've already used those smelly mothballs, or in fact have inherited a chest or suitcase from someone who did, it's time for the lemon to the rescue again. Wash the offending areas with lemon juice and water in equal quantities to rid your home of that really unpleasant odor.

Pop Some in the Wardrobe

To keep clothes and wardrobes smelling delicious, dry out some lemon peel. This may take several days, but once they're really dry put them in a small bowl in the wardrobe, or in the clothes drawer of your dresser.

Prevent Drains from Smelling

Pour a glass of water containing the juice of a whole lemon down the kitchen sink to keep it fresh-smelling. You can do the same for bath, shower and sink plugholes, because they can also smell, particularly in hot weather. The lemon juice will also disinfect as it travels down the drains.

Pop Some in the Vacuum Bag

Freshening as you work must be an added bonus. Sprinkle a few drops of lemon oil onto a piece of kitchen roll, then drop this into the bag of your vacuum cleaner. What a great way to freshen the air all over the house as you clean away the dirt and grime. If you don't have any lemon oil, then a couple of drops of lemon juice will have the same aromatic effect.

Freshen Carpets and Rugs

While you have the vacuum cleaner out, why not freshen up the carpets and rugs around the home? It does take a little forethought, but it is very effective. Mix together 10 drops of lemon oil, with an equal amount of one of your other favorite essential oils. Add this mixture of sweet-smelling oils to 125 g/4½ oz/1 cup of baking soda. Baking soda is really good at neutralizing smells and the oils provide long-lasting and sweet aromas.

Leave the mixture overnight to ensure that the baking soda has absorbed all of the oil and then liberally sprinkle it over your carpets and rugs. Let it soak into the tufts of the carpet or rug for a while and then vacuum up the mixture.

Eliminate Fireplace Odors

Picture the scene: the wind is howling outside, it is freezing cold and you are sitting beside a warm fire. Absolute joy! But then it starts to belch smoke and the whole room begins to smell like a bonfire! Absolute nightmare! To get rid of that really unpleasant, clogging smell, throw a few pieces of lemon peel into the fire.

You might want to remember to do this as a general rule each time you light the fire, because lemon peel is a good preventative measure against excess smoke. Add it to your firewood when you lay the fire and it will reduce the chance of it happening again.

Pot Pourri

When you buy pot pourri you often find that the smell only lasts for a short while. Why not try adding some dried lemon peel to your favorite dried leaves, flowers or shop-bought pot pourri. To keep it fresh add a few drops of lemon oil onto the peel regularly, or even a few drops of lemon juice will do the job.

Air Humidifier

If you have an air humidifier you'll know that they are really effective, but they can begin to smell a bit stagnant after a while. Add a few drops of lemon juice to the water in the humidifier to freshen it. The lemony aroma will circulate around the room as the machine does its job.

Holiday Lemons

Holiday Decorations

If you're looking for a project for the December holiday season, you could make your own decorations, using lemons of course. It needs a bit of advance planning, but this project would definitely make your tree unique. In about October, put several lemons in a dark cupboard to dry out, making sure you check them from time to time. You could also start to gather pieces of ribbon and pretty, glittering items to stick onto the dried lemons just before the holidays start.

When you're ready to adorn your tree, stick or pin your glittering items into the lemons. Stick a piece of ribbon onto each one to use for hanging and you'll have unique tree decorations!

Easier Holiday Decorations

If you aren't too good at pre-planning or you do not have the time, then you could just make some pomanders to hang. Stick a few cloves into fresh lemons and use ribbon to hang them. You don't have to put them on the tree, they could hang anywhere.

Everyday Decorations

Fresh lemons are such a vibrant color that they don't always need other items added to make them look attractive. Why not try placing some lemons in an unusually shaped, glass bowl. They look so striking you're sure to get compliments.

Pests & Garden

Baking soda, lemons and vinegar have a number of herbicidal and insecticidal uses, as well as being handy for certain gardening jobs. And because they are made from natural organic products you will not be harming the environment with chemicals. The vinegar that is available for household use does not normally exceed 5 per cent acetic acid, but stronger vinegars for use specifically as herbicides can be purchased. Solutions of over 10 per cent acidity can be 'corrosive' to skin, so make sure you handle them with care.

Greenhouses & Gardening

Wash Down

Some people use proprietary disinfectant fluid to clean their greenhouses in the autumn. However, if you want an ingredient that is just as effective, but cheaper, you can use baking soda. Wash all the surfaces, including the roof and walls, with baking soda and water. It will kill any mold and bacteria that may have formed during the growing season, as well as making the glass shine.

For an alternative mixture to wipe down the surfaces in your greenhouse and remove dirt and grime, mix 4 teaspoons baking soda with 120 ml/4 fl oz/½ cup white vinegar and 2.25 litres/4 pints/2¼ qts water. You can even put this mixture into a spray bottle, bit by bit, to make it easier to apply. Simply wipe off the dirt with a damp cloth.

Greenhouse Fungicide

Baking soda has been used for years as a mild fungicide, particularly by organic growers. It can be used against powdery mildew and other plant diseases in the greenhouse too. Mix 5 tablespoons baking soda with 4 litres/7 pints/4 qts water and spray the greenhouse and the affected plants.

Routine for Roses

No matter how careful a gardener you are, mold and mildew still spread really quickly once they take hold. To keep mold on plants, particularly roses, at bay you can spray with a mixture of 100 g/7 oz/1 cup baking soda and 2.25 litres/4 pints/2¼ qts water. It certainly stops the mold from spreading to other plants.

Clean the Bottle

When you've sprayed your garden plants, be sure to kill any mildew or fungus inside the spray nozzle. Add a little baking soda and this should do the job for you. Also, before you put your sprayer into storage do the same thing so it's fresh when watering time comes around again.

Defeat Disease

You can mix 4 teaspoons baking soda into 7.5 litres/11¾ pints/7½ qts water to treat diseased plants. Apply the mixture generously to the diseased plants with a hand-held spray. You will have to fill the spray several times, but do make sure you cover all the diseased parts of the plant, including the foliage.

Also, cider vinegar can help rust, black spot and powdery mildew. Mix 1 tablespoon apple cider vinegar with 1 litre/2 pints/4½ cups water and decant into a spray bottle. Spray the vinegar solution onto the affected plants in the early morning or early evening when the temperature is relatively cool and there is no direct sunlight on the plants. Repeat until the condition is cured.

Free the Lawn from Mold

If your lawn needs some serious attention there's no better way to give it a boost than baking soda, particularly if you have problems with mold. Use 1 tablespoon to 4 litres/7 pints/4 qts water and spray the lawn, or you can apply it with a watering can. It kills off mold or mildew without having to use a fungicide and gives the lawn a bit of a tonic.

Another way of spreading the baking soda on to your lawn is to fill a sock or an old pair of tights with some neat baking soda. Beat the side of the sock or the tights with your hands to release the dust. You get more of an even spread this way and you can always water it in with a hose if it doesn't rain.

Sweeter Tomatoes

Tomato plants like baking soda too! Sprinkle a little around their roots regularly from the first planting. The baking soda will reduce their acidity and make them even sweeter to eat.

Improve Soil Quality

There are lots of bags of compost available in garden centers, but many people choose to make their own. If you make your own organic compost you will realize it is much better for your garden soil than those that contain chemicals. The secret to good-quality soil is good-quality compost. Adding citrus fruit to the compost can help improve soil quality enormously because it enriches the soil with nutrients. The lemon, orange or grapefruit will help to regulate the flow of water and oxygen to the roots of the plants. This will obviously give you a healthier plant, which will also be less prone to pests and diseases.

Acid or Alkaline?

Some plants like an acid soil, some like it alkaline and some – like weeds – just do not seem to care either way. Find out if your garden soil is alkaline by placing a handful of soil in to a container, and then pour on 120 ml/4 fl oz/½ cup white vinegar. If the soil fizzes or bubbles, your soil is alkaline. If you have a large garden, try the test using soil from different spots to see if it is alkaline throughout. To test for an acid soil, mix a handful of soil with 120 ml/4 fl oz/½ cup water and 2 heaped tablespoons baking soda. Any fizzing and bubbling this time tells you that your soil is acid. While you now know what kind of soil you have, to find out the exact pH levels, you will need a simple testing kit from a garden center.

Increase Soil Acidity

Some plants, such as azaleas, gardenias, hydrangeas and rhododendrons, thrive in acid soils. Keep an eye out for yellowing leaves on these plants as this could be signaling a lack of iron or a shift in the soil's pH level above 5.0. If you live in a hard water area, the acidity levels in your soil might be low. To bring the acidity to a comfortable level for these plants, add 230 ml/8 fl oz/1 cup white vinegar to a each large bucket of tap water, and water once a week for three weeks. The acetic acid in the vinegar will release the iron in the soil for the plants' use.

Blooming Marvellous

After cutting flowers from the garden to take into the house, why not try dipping their stems in a mild baking soda and water mix? It will help the flowers to stay fresh longer and kills any bacteria on the stems.

It has been believed for many years that applying proprietary lemonade to pot plants will help ensure they flower for longer. Since then many people also put their cut flowers into lemonade. But you can use fresh lemon juice, too. Try adding 2 tbsp of lemon juice to the water in your vase, together with 1 tbsp of sugar next time you arrange your cut flowers. It does make a difference to the amount of time they stay fresh.

CAUTION: Do not add lemonade or lemon juice to chrysanthemums as this can turn the leaves of the flowers brown.

Alternatively, place into your vase 2 tablespoons sugar and 2 tablespoons white vinegar for each litre/2 pints/4½ cups water. Trim the flower stems and change the 'feed' every four to five days.

Speed Up Sprouting

Some seeds, especially the woody seeds of plants such as gourds, passionflowers and morning glory can be given a helping hand to germinate if you rub them gently between two sheets of fine sandpaper and then soak them overnight in a solution of 600 ml/1 pint/2½ cups warm water and 120 ml/4 fl oz/½ cup apple cider vinegar. The next morning, take the seeds out of the solution, rinse them off, and plant them. Herb seeds can also be difficult to get started, and the same technique – but without the sandpaper massage – will help.

Pest Control

Ants No More!

Ants – whoever needs them? Although they don't do much damage they are still off-putting, particularly if they are near your doors and windows. You can sprinkle neat baking soda around their entrance and exit areas to help get rid of them and hopefully stop them getting into the house.

Ants also seem to love children's sandboxes. If they are invading your child's sandbox, then mix a whole box of baking soda well into the sand. That should keep them away!

Ants don't like lemon either, and the most effective way to rid your house of them is to use a rotten lemon. Place a whole, rotten lemon close to the entrance point they are using to get into your home. You can also squirt your doorways and windowsills with lemon juice, particularly if you can identify where they are entering the house. This organic DIY repellent is also effective against cockroaches and fleas.

Ants also hate the scent of vinegar, so pour or spray white vinegar around an 'exclusion zone' and they'll stay clear.

Fleeing Fleas

Fleas don't like baking soda either. You can sprinkle it on your lawn, where they often congregate, believe it or not. Or you can sprinkle the baking soda directly on to your pet to make sure they don't stay on too long either.

Clear out Cockroaches

Cockroaches seem to like damp places and places where water settles. You don't want cockroaches in your home because they spread so many germs. Try and keep damp areas free of the little devils, particularly around water pipes and in cellars, by sprinkling neat baking soda in these areas.

Repel Rabbits

No matter how sweet we think they are, rabbits can do a lot of damage in the garden. They can be particularly harmful to plants that have been recently planted and especially to lettuce and cabbages. To ward off rabbits, sprinkle some baking soda generously around the vegetable patch.

Say No to Slugs and Snails

Slugs and snails can do even more damage than rabbits. They can destroy a newly planted vegetable or bedding plant overnight by eating the sweet leaves. At least if you use the baking soda generously you should be able to deter most of these pests in one fell swoop. And your plants might actually feed you.

Natural Insecticide

It may seem strange, but the majority of insects really do not like the smell of lemon. But you do need to be thorough in your application of the lemon juice and peel. Make sure you squeeze liberal amounts of lemon juice on doorsteps and windowsills, as well as any obvious cracks or gaps in the brickwork where you think they could get into the house.

You could also put cut strips of lemon peel around your doorways – why not try the juice and the peel if you really hate creepy crawlies?

Deter Unwelcome House Guests

If you've got insects inside the house, and this usually means in the kitchen, perhaps even inside your cupboards, then reach for the lemon again. The limonene in the lemon is toxic to insects, so wipe your surfaces or cupboards with either lemon oil or juice to get rid of them.

Get Rid of Houseflies

We all know how much bacteria the common housefly is capable of spreading around our houses. There is nothing worse than seeing one crawling over kitchen worktops. If you use lemon juice regularly to clean your work surfaces then this will help keep the germ-spreading insects at bay.

A 'Friendly' Fly Trap

Gnats, midges, flies and mosquitoes can all be shown the door using a simple organic trap. Take an empty plastic water or pop bottle and pour in around 120 ml/4 fl oz/½ cup apple cider vinegar, about 4 tablespoons sugar, and 120 ml/4 fl oz/½ cup water. Next, cut up a banana skin into small pieces and put them in the solution and shake well. You can either tie a piece of string around the neck of the bottle and hang it from a tree branch, or place it on the ground: either way hungry flies will make a beeline for the free lunch inside, but have great trouble exiting the neck of the bottle once there.

Eliminate those Moths!

If you think you might have moths in the wardrobe then don't resort to smelly mothballs. Instead place a small bag of dried lemon peel in the wardrobe. It will help get rid of them.

Insect-free Paintwork

It has happened to all of us. You're outside giving your home a fresh coat of paint in the summer. You use white gloss paint for the woodwork and you go inside for a coffee only to find on your return that your shiny, white paintwork is covered with tiny bugs and insects. They've stuck to the drying paint. Next time you need to paint outside try rubbing down the door frames or other surfaces you intend to paint with some lemon juice first. It will help keep those little midges away while your paint is drying.

Squirrel Repellent

Lemon juice, and some say hot, spicy foods like chili peppers, can be spread in areas that neighborhood squirrels frequent regularly. Try placing grated lemon peel around your bird-feeders. They don't like the taste so it will deter them from returning.

If squirrels are causing damage to your flowerbeds, liberally sprinkle grated lemon peel around your plants. It won't hurt the plants but it will stop the squirrels from bothering them.

Deter Visiting Cats and Others

Cats do not like the smell of citrus fruit, so using lemon or orange peel in your garden is an effective repellent. Grate and sprinkle liberal amounts of lemon peel where those visiting cats tend to frequent your garden and that should send them back home again.

There are many visitors to our gardens who are more than welcome, but there are some whom we wish would stay away. Many animals, including cats, rabbits and deer, cannot stand the smell of vinegar even when it is dry. So to stop neighbors' cats using your borders as a lavatory, and rabbits and deer dining on your vegetable patch, soak some rags in neat white vinegar, and tie them to some sticks or staves. Once a week, soak the rags in vinegar again to keep up the scent.

Train Your Own Cat

If you have a new kitten, or have acquired a stray cat, it is likely that certain parts of your home will be out of bounds for them. Mix some lemon juice and water in a spray bottle and spray it in the areas that you want the cat to avoid. You might have to do this regularly so that they learn.

Get Rid of Mealy bugs

Mealy bugs are one of the most common pests to be found on houseplants and in the greenhouse, where they feast on plant juices and can cause leaf drop and subsequent plant death. Look under the leaves and at the junctions with the stem: if you see these small scaly insects, then dab them with a cotton wool ball soaked in white vinegar. The vinegar will kill them – and any eggs they may have laid.

Banish Weeds

Dandelions spoiling your lawn? Banish them by spraying with undiluted white vinegar. Break off the flower head and spray the stalk and around the base of the plant in order to soak the roots. If it rains in the night, go out and spray again! The same treatment also works well for getting rid of grass on driveways and paths.

Lemon is also good for killing garden weeds. That doesn't mean you are likely to rid your whole garden of them, but lemon juice doused along cracks in pathways and patios will work.

CAUTION: Do not douse any of your garden plants directly with lemon juice as this could harm them.

Pet Care

Having healthy and well-behaved pets is probably as important to most pet owners as their own health. Of course you can buy many pet-care products that probably do work, but they can be expensive and you don't always know what ingredients they contain. Natural and easily available baking soda, lemon and vinegar give you lots of options for protecting your pet's health, and can be useful in different methods of training – not to mention dealing with the unique aroma of wet dogs, cat litter and hamster cages!

Clean Pets

Washing, Wet or Dry

Give your pooch a quick dry-clean by sprinkling him (or her, of course) with a little baking soda and brushing it through the coat. Probably best done in the garden, this will absorb grease and remove those doggy smells you don't want to smell.

For a wet wash, add a couple of tablespoons of baking soda to the water when you bath your dog. This solution can be used by itself, when it will also help heal any skin conditions, or with a dash of shampoo. You won't need to use as much shampoo as usual, as the addition of baking soda makes it work much more effectively. Rinse thoroughly after shampooing.

A Cleaner Vacuum Cleaner

Every time you change the bag on your vacuum cleaner pop in 1 tablespoon baking soda. And if it's the bagless type just drop the baking soda into the dirt collection chamber. This will quickly curb that less-than-fresh smell that can linger when the cleaner starts to get full, especially if you have a dog in the house.

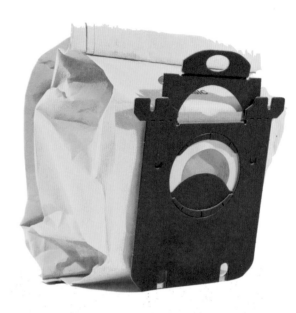

Whoops

When man's best friend leaves a nasty whiff on the carpet, sprinkle on some baking soda. Leave it for half an hour then vacuum up. The baking soda will also help stop those doggy smells gathering in your vacuum cleaner.

Worse Than Whoops

After a night on the town, or swallowing too much fur, your cat can sometimes be sick and will seldom, if ever, use the litter box. Wherever your cat decides to throw up, a solution of baking soda and water will not only clean up the mess, it should also remove any stains and unpleasant smells.

The Worst

Should one of your pets leave something unspeakable on the carpet, scrape up or dry up as much as you can, then scrub the whole area with a solution of baking soda and warm water. Sprinkle the area liberally with more baking soda and leave overnight, vacuuming up any residue the next day. Getting rid of that telltale smell quickly will discourage the little darlings from soiling the same spot repeatedly.

And So to Bed

Pet's beds and bedding can get dirty and start to smell. Freshen up your pet's sleeping arrangements by sprinkling with baking soda, leaving for at least 10 minutes, then vacuuming. Be sure to remove Fido first!

Blanket the Smell

Pet blankets can be home to some particularly powerful odors that even a good hot wash won't always shift. Bring your blankets back to smell-free cleanliness by adding 100 g/4 oz/½ cup baking soda to the detergent, either for machine or hand washing.

Alternatively, add 230 ml/8 fl oz/1 cup white vinegar to the cycle to deodorize and kill bacteria. Dogs and cats can, like their owners, suffer from sensitive skin: the vinegar will remove any remains of soap from their bedding to which they may be sensitive.

Kitty Litter

With the best will in the world, most us don't manage to clean out litter boxes quite as often as we should. Luckily, baking soda will absorb those telltale cat litter odors if you plan ahead. Next time you change your cat's box, cover the bottom with a layer of baking soda and then sprinkle the cat litter on top. Be generous with the baking soda: the best arrangement is a ratio of around one part baking soda to four parts of litter. Add a little extra baking soda each time you remove anything between changes.

Cat litter boxes tend to get a layer of scale in the base. Try using a mixture of white vinegar, water and freshly squeezed lemon juice in the cat box next time you clean it. Use 3 parts water to 1 part white vinegar and the juice of 2 lemons. Transfer this mixture to a spray bottle and after you've emptied and washed the box with warm, soapy water, spray the base of it with the mixture. Then scrub the base with a stiff brush, wash again and rinse the box thoroughly. The sediment will come off easily and the box will stay fresher for longer.

CAUTION: Do make sure you clean off the lemon thoroughly, as cats are not keen on the smell of lemon and you don't want to deter them from using the box.

White-collar Pets

Dogs' collars and leashes can get grimy and greasy over time, so scrub with a solution of baking soda and warm water. Nylon collars and leashes can be soaked in the solution if you prefer. This also works well on those plastic toys that your pet loves gnawing on.

How Clean Is Your Cage?

Next time you clean out a small pet's cage, sprinkle a layer of baking soda on the bottom before covering with a layer of newspaper, then bedding. Tank-style cages can be washed out with a solution of baking soda and warm water and rinsed in the bath or shower.

Feathered Friends

Birds can get salmonella and other similar gastric problems if you don't keep their feed hoppers and drinking containers spotless. Wash these carefully in a hot water and baking soda solution and rinse and dry carefully before replacing. Use the same solution, rather than strong-smelling detergent, to clean out the cage.

Alternatively, try vinegar. Empty out any leftovers from seed holders and immerse them in a bucket of hot water and 230 ml/8 fl oz/1 cup white vinegar. Let them sit in the bucket until the water is cold, then rinse really well with cold water. For bird fountains, pour in a solution of 2 parts white vinegar and 1 part hot water and if possible, give the inside a good scrub. Empty out the solution and rinse really well with clean water.

Dinner is Served

While dogs tend to eat their food in one sitting, cats like to graze. In either case, their dinner bowls can often hold the scent of their food, so after every feed, wash their bowls, then deodorize them with a solution of equal parts white vinegar and water and rinse well in clean water. Remember that cats loathe the smell of vinegar, so make sure Kitty's bowl is well rinsed.

Thanks for All the Fish (Tank)

Fish don't like it if their water becomes too acidic, so test the water with a special kit regularly and add a pinch or so of baking soda to correct the level if necessary. And when you need to clean the tank, baking soda and water in paste form is perfect for scrubbing it out. It's safe and leaves no taint. Make sure you rinse the tank out carefully before refilling.

Healthy Happy Pets

Lemon Spray for Dogs

Lemon is very effective for conditioning a dog's coat and keeping your pet flea free. Add slices of lemon to ½ litre/1 pint/2 cups of boiling water and leave the mixture to cool by letting it stand overnight. Strain the mixture and then pour it into a spray bottle. You can spray your animal liberally with this mixture without it having any harmful effects. The limonene in the lemon conditions the dog's coat and it is also an effective repellent for flies and other flying insects. This spray is also very effective for keeping away animal fleas. These unwanted little creatures have a waxy coating. When the liquid is sprayed onto the animal's fur it disables the flea from feeding.

CAUTION: Avoid spraying the lemon juice mixture near to the dog's eyes.

Tick Tactics

Fill a spray-bottle with equal parts of water and white vinegar and apply directly to your pet's coat, rubbing it in well. This may take some doing with a cat because they absolutely hate the smell of vinegar, but then it seems, so do the ticks and fleas!

Hear Kitty Kitty!

If your cat – or dog – has been scratching at their ears more than usual, a clean-out with a ball of cotton wool or a soft cloth dabbed in a dilute solution of 2 parts apple cider vinegar and 1 part water will clean them and deter ear mites. Warning: do make a visual inspection of your pet's ear first; do not apply the vinegar even in dilute form to open scratches or sores.

Protect Dog's Ears from Damage While Swimming

If your dog is a keen swimmer, the chances are that water in the ears might be or has been a problem. You can protect your pet's ears by using a lemon flush. Mix together the juice of half a lemon with some warm water. You will need to use an ear dropper, or even a syringe, to administer the mixture. Gently squeeze some of the liquid into each of your pet's ears and, again gently, massage the outside of the ear to rub it in. Your pet will probably have a good shake at this stage, at which point you can blot away the excess moisture with cotton wool or a cotton bud.

CAUTION: Do not place the syringe or ear dropper right inside your pet's ear canal as the squirting noise might frighten it and the ear canal is very delicate.

Train Your Dog to Stop Barking

You can buy anti-barking collars that contain citronella. These squirt into the dog's face every time it barks to deter it from excessive barking. However it is much cheaper and probably just as effective to make your own version using a water pistol or spray bottle and some lemon juice. Fill the water pistol or spray bottle with water and add a few drops of lemon juice. The spray isn't meant to be a punishment but is meant to startle the dog into silence by interrupting the barking. Every time the dog barks you spray the lemon mixture into his or her mouth and praise when the barking stops. If the barking begins again, repeat the process.

CAUTION: Do not spray the lemon juice and water mixture directly into the dog's face and be careful to avoid the eyes.

Stop Puppies from Biting Your Hands

Because dogs do not like the taste of lemon, you could try rubbing lemon juice into your hands if you have one that likes to gnaw your fingers. It might take two or three goes before your puppy realizes, but it will stop them biting your hands eventually.

Pet Potty Training

Housebreaking a kitten or a puppy needs patience – and vinegar – as they will wet any previously spoiled spots because it is marked with their scent. As well as cleaning up, it is vital to remove the scent from the floor, carpet or upholstery. For carpets, rugs and upholstery, blot up as much of the stain as possible with paper towels, then pour undiluted white vinegar over the spot and blot again. Reapply the vinegar, blot and let it air dry. For wood and vinyl floors, test an inconspicuous area with a solution of equal parts white vinegar and water to make sure it does not damage the floor's finish. If satisfactory, mop the floor and dry with a cloth or paper towel. In both instances the vinegar will remove the scent so the place will not be 'marked' again.

You can also try spraying the area with neat lemon juice, which won't hurt your floor or carpet. The smell will eliminate the odor in your home and will also deter the animal from returning to its own scent.

This is NOT a scratching post!

By the same token, since cats absolutely hate the smell of vinegar, even after it has dried, a little neat, white vinegar dabbed onto the proposed scratching post will thwart them!

An Apple a Day...

Vinegar is acid until it enters the body, where it becomes alkaline and lines the intestines where bacteria such as E. Coli can no longer attach themselves. A teaspoon of apple cider vinegar added to your dogs' drinking water will keep their insides in top condition.

Bites and Stings

Dab a dilute solution of apple cider vinegar and water onto bee stings and mosquito bites to relieve itching.

Health &
Personal Care

Beauty Tips

Baking soda can be used in so many different ways to improve appearance, from alleviating irritating little rashes to making your skin so healthy-looking that people will believe you have used one of the luxury brands. All parts of a lemon contain something that we can use to make ourselves look and feel beautiful – lemons can cleanse, moisturize and help maintain the pH balance in skin. Meanwhile, the astringent and toning qualities of vinegar – particularly apple cider vinegar – can reduce inflammation, redness, bruising and swelling.

Skin

Ease Razor Burn

When we talk about razor burn we automatically think of men shaving their face. But you can get razor burn on your legs or under your armpits too and that really can be just as uncomfortable for women as facial razor burn is for men. Once again a baking soda paste can come to the rescue quite quickly. Make the paste quite a thin one and dab it onto the area affected by the razor burn to get almost immediate relief from the burning sensation.

However, if that doesn't work quite as quickly as you'd like then you could sprinkle neat baking soda on to the skin.

Exfoliate

Mixing a paste of three parts baking soda to one part water is a brilliant way of exfoliating the body and getting rid of those dead skin cells. It is also really inexpensive and easy to use. The same quantities can be mixed to a paste and applied to the face as a facial scrub. Use it after washing for that freshly scrubbed feeling. Apply the facial scrub in a circular movement to the face and then rinse it off with cool water.

Or you can try lemons: cut a lemon in half and dip it into ordinary white sugar. Using this as your

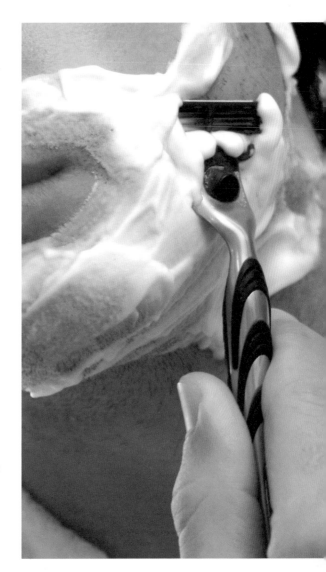

exfoliator, gently rub your face to remove the build up of dead skin. If you do this regularly you'll notice the difference. The lemon juice is really good at loosening dead skin cells and the sugar acts as a mild abrasive. Do it at bedtime though, so you don't risk being in the sunlight immediately afterwards.

For a more through exfoliation, prepare in advance a mixture of 225 g/8 oz/¾ cup of sea salt with ½ tbsp of lemon oil and put it beside the bath. Draw yourself a warm bath. Rub your damp skin with the lemon-scented salt. This will deal with dead skin cells and give your skin a smooth and healthy glow.

You could try adding coconut oil or almond oil in addition to the lemon oil to give you a really sumptuous-smelling body scrub for the bath.

CAUTION: If you have any skin sensitivity, try a test patch for any lemon treatments first, as they are quite acidic and can dry or irritate skin.

Pen Stains on Fingertips

You know when an ink, ballpoint or felt-tip pen decides to leak all over your fingers? Well, an easy way to remove this type of stain is to rub your hands together with a mix of baking soda and water. Rub away at the stain with confidence that it will not affect your skin but it will remove the stain. It will also remove some paint stains.

Hand Moisturizer

Remember the advertisement that went 'Now hands that do dishes can feel soft as your face'? Well that can be true of any washday red hands if you add a little baking soda into your dishwashing water. The baking soda softens your hands, no matter how long you have to stand at the kitchen sink.

Rough Patches

Those little parts of your body that seem to acquire hard skin for no particular reason, for example the elbows and knees, will definitely benefit from a baking soda paste. Mix to a paste and rub into the affected area to leave the skin feeling softer. It works on the soles and heels of the feet as well.

Baking Soda Bath Salts

Lying in a hot bath when your body is aching from exertion must be one of the nicest feelings. But you don't have to pay expensive prices to buy salts to add to the bath. Mix equal quantities of sea salt and baking soda (about 200 g/7 oz/1 cup is fine for one bath) and 250 ml/8 fl oz/1 cup of the shampoo of your choice while the water is running. Once the bath is half-full add your mixture and then top the bath up with more water. You'll get some bubbles if you swirl your hand around and then you can soak to your heart's content.

Baking Soda Bath Oil

Making bath oil out of baking soda is just as easy as making bath salts, but this time you should let the bath fill completely before adding the mixture. Use the following ingredients and mix them in advance of your bath time, but don't attempt to keep any over for the next one – they have to be used fresh. In a mixing bowl add 225 g/8 oz/1 cup sea salt, 4 tablespoons baking soda, 250 ml/8 fl oz/1 cup honey and 450 ml/16 fl oz/1¾ cups milk. Once the bath is full, pour the mixture in and add 115 ml/4 fl oz/½ cup of any of your favorite proprietary baby oil. This will give your skin a lovely soft and silky feel and you are sure to feel nicely relaxed too.

Dry Skin Bath Additive

If you are suffering with dry skin from the central heating or because of an allergy, you can relieve this by mixing 100 g/4 oz/½ cup baking soda, 75 g/3 oz/1 cup oatmeal, 250 ml/8 fl oz/1 cup warm water and 1 tablespoon vanilla essence (or your favorite) into a paste. Let the mixture run under the tap while you are running your bath. It certainly stops the itching.

Apple Cider Vinegar Soft Skin

Apple cider vinegar added to a soaking bath – or even vinegar-soaked 'bandages' wrapped around knees and elbows and left on overnight – are the 'lazy way' to deal with rough or hard skin. In the morning, bathe as usual and gently rub the dry areas with a pumice stone in small circular motions to remove dead skin.

Body Massage

In addition to all the other wonderful things we've learned about, lemons are also believed to help the skin's elasticity and discourage cellulite. Try mixing equal amounts of honey, vegetable oil and lemon juice together. Use this as your massage oil and pay particular attention to those areas of the

body that are particularly dry. Leave the mixture on your body for about 10 minutes before rinsing it off in the shower or a warm bath.

Cleansing

Lemons have a strong reputation for being particularly good at cleansing and they also have clarifying properties. Lemon juice can help remove dead skin cells and stimulate collagen production. You could use this lemon cleansing treatment every day to remove the dirt and grime that has built up on your face. Squeeze the juice from half a lemon into a bowl and apply to your face with your fingertips. Gently massage the lemon juice into your pores and then rinse your face.

CAUTION: Do not cleanse the area around the eyes with lemon juice, as this could cause stinging.

Deep Cleansing

Lemons are particularly useful for combatting greasy skin as they are great for unclogging pores. The lemon oil helps to balance overactive sebaceous glands, which are often what cause greasy skin, blocked pores and skin blemishes. One good method of deep cleansing to make sure those pores are cleaned thoroughly is to steam the face. Fill a bowl with boiling water and add the peel of half a lemon. With your face over the bowl and a tea towel over your head, let the lemony steam penetrate the pores. You'll be amazed at how refreshing this feels, too!

Toning

Once you've cleansed your face you'll want to tone it to close those pores up again. Use two parts ice-cold water to one part lemon juice to tone after cleansing. Apply the cold toner to clean skin and allow it to dry naturally. Can you imagine how good this toner makes you feel on a really hot day? You can store this cold, lemony toner in the refrigerator for several days.

CAUTION: Do not be tempted to go into the sunshine after using lemon on the face because the lemon juice can react to the sun's UV rays and burn or blemish the skin.

The use of vinegar as a skin toner dates back to the ancient Egyptians. After cleaning your face, rinse with a basin of cool water with 1 tablespoon apple cider vinegar. You will notice any residual grease from make-up and make-up removers is removed and your skin is cooled, toned and feels a little 'tighter'.

CAUTION: Take care not to get the solution in your eyes: if you accidentally splash it in your eyes, rinse out with cold water.

Toning Oily Skin

For oily skin, mix 2 tbsp of lemon juice, 2 tbsp of vodka, 1 tbsp of distilled water and 1 tsp of witch hazel. Use a cotton wool pad to apply this toner to your skin and then rinse your face with water. This toner will also keep for around a week if stored in the refrigerator.

Wrinkle Reducers

Lemons can be used in a number of different ways to help improve the appearance of wrinkles. One of the simplest methods is to stir a teaspoon of sugar into 2 tbsp of lemon juice. Massage this solution into your skin using your fingertips. Leave the mix on your face for 10 minutes before rinsing off with water. This treatment

will exfoliate the skin, but the Vitamin C in the lemon will also promote the production of collagen. Acids in the sugar will help repair skin damage and also remove dead skin.

Another homemade remedy for wrinkles and fine lines on the face is to mix together 1 tsp of tomato juice, ½ tsp of lemon juice and a pinch of turmeric. Form this into a paste with gram or chickpea flour. Apply the paste to the wrinkled area, and leave for 15 to 20 minutes before washing off.

Using lemon juice as an essential ingredient for a facial mask also helps reduce wrinkles. Add 1 tbsp of lemon juice to a well-beaten egg white and 1 tsp of egg yolk. Add a drop of Vitamin E oil into this mix and form a paste. Apply the paste to the skin and leave for 30 minutes before washing off. Moisturize your face after you have used this wrinkle treatment.

One further anti-wrinkle treatment requires a little more time and preparation. You will need several lemons, two cucumbers, whipped cream, olive oil, honey and cornstarch. Slice the unpeeled cucumbers and put them into a blender, together with the whipped cream, and blitz until you have a paste. Add a drop or two of olive oil and honey and continue blitzing before adding just a pinch of cornstarch. Now put the mixture into the refrigerator and let it chill for at least 30 minutes. When you are ready for this luxurious anti-wrinkle treatment, cut the lemons in half and begin rubbing them generously but lightly over your neck and face. Don't dry the skin and apply the paste mixture straightaway. Leave the mix to do its job for at least an hour before rinsing it off.

Pimple and Blackhead Solutions

Spots and pimples are caused by excess sebum (the natural oil excreted by the skin's sebaceous glands) that blocks up the pores and hair follicles, leading to blackheads and whiteheads. Lemon juice is an excellent astringent and it can help remove dirt that can clog your pores. We all know that clogged pores can cause blackheads and pimples, but there are natural ways that lemons can help.

Squeeze the juice of half a lemon into a small bowl, then dip a cotton wool ball into the juice and dab it onto your face, taking care to avoid your eyes. You can either leave it on for around 10 minutes before washing it off, or you can do this just before you go to bed at night. Leave the lemon juice to soak in overnight before rinsing off in the morning. The citric acid in the lemon juice will naturally dissolve the oils that conspire to create blackheads. See below for a useful regular facial mask to treat blackheads.

Apple cider vinegar can help clear the complexion by balancing the skin's pH level and absorbing excess oil from the skin. A dilute solution of 1 part apple cider vinegar and 3 to 4 parts water applied three times a day to the skin and left there for 10 minutes or so before rinsing off will help clear the complexion.

Cleansing Facial Masks

Here are two simple recipes to create easy-to-use cleansing masks with lemon as one of the main ingredients.

As a regular treatment for blackheads mix 2 tbsp of oatmeal with 4 tbsp of plain yogurt, and 1 tbsp of lemon juice. Mix the ingredients into a paste and apply to the skin. Leave this cleansing facial mask on for at least five minutes, then rinse off with cold water. Either pat the face dry or leave it to air dry naturally.

For deep cleansing, mix 4 tbsp of plain yogurt with 2 tbsp of grated lemon peel. Massage this mask into your skin and leave on the face for up to five minutes, then rinse off with warm water. During this deep cleanse the lemon peel dissolves the dirt and oil and the yogurt exfoliates your skin.

Dark Spots Lightener

'Age spots' or 'liver spots' can be caused by hormonal changes and over-exposure to the sun. Lemon juice is one of the most natural and potent skin-bleaching products available. Squeeze a lemon into a small container or spray bottle. Dilute the lemon juice with an equal amount of water. Optionally you can add a drop of honey or aloe vera oil, as these are both useful moisturizers.

Apply the lemon mixture to a test area first, such as the neck, and then rinse it off. If the test patch proves to be problem free then apply the mixture to the darker spots you wish to lighten. Leave the mixture on for a minute or two before rinsing off with water. Make sure you then moisturize your skin well. You can repeat this treatment weekly.

Alternatively, try mixing 1 tbsp of yogurt with a drop or two of lemon juice. Apply the mixture directly to the age spot and leave for 10 minutes before rinsing off.

An alternative treatment is to simply dab fresh lemon juice directly onto the age spots twice a day. Leave the juice on the skin for as long as you like and you should notice improvements after around two months of daily treatment. Again, try a test patch first.

Age spots and sun spots can also be successfully remedied by dabbing with full-strength apple cider vinegar applied with a cotton wool ball for about ten minutes twice a day. Often the spots will fade in a few weeks, but if they worry you or you notice any significant increase in size or darkness, consult your medical practitioner.

CAUTION: Using lemon juice in its concentrated form could irritate sensitive skins. It can also dry the skin, so it is important to moisturize after use. If the lemon juice stings the skin you should rinse it off immediately and remember not to go straight into the sunlight.

Skin Brightener

As lemons have their own fruit acids, sugar and are rich in enzymes, they are great for getting rid of dead skin cells. Simply slice a lemon and gently rub it onto the face. This will tone and refresh the skin. Wash off the lemon juice after this treatment.

Shiny Face Reducer

Brush your face with lemon juice using a clean makeup brush. Leave the juice on your skin for five minutes before rinsing off. The lemon juice will help deal with the over production of oil in the skin. As an alternative, use 120 ml/4 fl oz/½ cup of water mixed with 10 drops of lemon juice. Using a cotton wool ball, dab the mixture all over the face.

CAUTION: If you are using neat lemon juice do this last thing at night, as the lemon juice may cause a temporary redness of the skin.

Broken Veins and Bruises

As a gentle astringent, apple cider vinegar is a useful treatment for those tiny, but unsightly broken veins that can often appear on the surface of skin. Dab on undiluted apple cider vinegar to speed the repair and reduce redness. Bruises can also be treated in the same way.

Dark Underarms and Elbows

We've already seen how lemon juice can help reduce dark patches on the skin. If you have discolored elbows or dark patches of skin under the armpit then lemons can also help. For elbows, cut a lemon in half and rest your elbows in each half for 10 minutes. Rinse off with warm water.

For discolored armpits cut a thick slice of lemon and clamp your arm against your body, trapping the lemon slice. Leave for 10 minutes. Rinse off with warm water. You can repeat both of these treatments regularly until the darker skin gradually lightens.

Hair & Nails

Hair Shampoo

You can make your own homemade shampoo with lemon juice as the vital ingredient. Mix a whole egg with 1 tsp of olive oil, 1 tsp of lemon juice, 120 ml/4 fl oz/½ cup of warm water and a few small pieces of your favorite soap, or a squirt of liquid soap. If you are using pieces of soap, soak them in the warm water until they are soft before adding the remaining ingredients.

Your homemade shampoo will last for up to three days, and even longer if it is kept in the refrigerator.

Hair Conditioner

There are at least a couple of ways of making your own hair conditioner using lemons. If you have dull or damaged hair, mix together 3 tbsp of lemon juice, 120 ml/4 fl oz/½ cup of honey and 200 ml/7 fl oz/¾ cup of olive oil. Shampoo your hair as normal and then towel dry. Apply the mixture to your hair and comb it through. Cover your hair with a plastic cap and leave for 30 minutes. Then shampoo and rinse your hair as normal.

For a more general hair conditioner, use one egg, the juice of half a lemon, 1 tbsp of olive oil and 3 tbsp of henna powder. Beat the egg until it is frothy, then slowly add the henna powder and the lemon juice. You may need to add a few drops of water at this stage if the mixture feels

too stiff. Allow the mixture to set for an hour before using it. Apply to your hair and scalp, and leave it on for an hour before rinsing and shampooing.

Sometimes if you use the same shampoo or mousse all the time, you can get a build-up on your hair, making it feel lank, greasy, drab and lifeless. By adding 2 teaspoons baking soda to a teaspoon of your favorite shampoo and mixing them together you can help to condition your hair and remove the build-up. You just have to wash and then rinse your hair as normal with your mixture. This mix gives your hair a good shine and leaves it feeling really clean.

Bring the life back into limp or damaged hair with a nourishing apple cider vinegar hair conditioner. Whip together 1 teaspoon apple cider vinegar with 2 tablespoons almond or olive oil and 3 egg whites. Gently massage the mix into your hair then cover with a shower cap – or plastic wrap – for 30 minutes. Rinse with warm – not hot – water, unless you want scrambled egg whites cooked in your hair! Then shampoo and wash as normal.

Hairbrushes and Combs

How embarrassing is it when someone asks you if they can borrow one of your hairbrushes or combs and they look absolutely filthy, or even if they are visible when visitors appear at your home? It can't be avoided easily because of hair, dirt and grime, but why not try boiling them (if they are of a suitable material) for about 10 minutes in water and baking soda? Just add 200 g/7 oz/1 cup baking soda to the water and boil the dirt and grime away.

Sun-Kissed Hair

Lemons are natural bleaching agents. All you need to do is to squeeze the juice of half to a whole lemon straight onto your hair. Sit out in the sun for at least 30 minutes and then shampoo and condition your hair as normal. Alternatively, mix 4 tbsp of lemon juice with 175 ml/6 fl oz/¾ cup of water, then rinse your clean, wet hair with the mixture. Sit out in the sun until your hair dries.

If you are light haired, blonde highlights will begin to appear. If you are darker haired, then you will see red tones begin to appear in the hair.

Shiny Hair

This treatment is particularly effective if you have greasy hair. After you have shampooed, rinse with a little water and the juice of half a lemon. The lemon's natural acidity will counteract the alkaline traces of the shampoo. It will also dissolve any residual soap and help to create fatty acids that will give your hair a natural shine.

Treating Damaged or Colored Hair

Bleaches and coloring agents can often damage your hair. Rinsing with water and the juice of half a lemon encourages natural proteins, which can counteract hair damage.

Blonde hair – whether natural or by design – can need extra protection especially if you swim in chlorinated pools. The chlorine keeps the water safe but it can give blonde hair a greenish tinge so to protect it, rub apple cider vinegar into your hair and let it set for 15 minutes or so before taking the plunge.

Help With Dandruff

There are two ways that lemons can rid you of an itching scalp and embarrassing dandruff flakes on the shoulders. Try adding 2 tbsp of lemon juice to 120 ml/4 fl oz/½ cup of olive oil. Gently rub the mixture onto your scalp and leave it for about 15 minutes before rinsing off. Then you can shampoo and condition your hair as normal.

Alternatively, mix a few drops of lemon juice into an egg white. Apply the mixture to your scalp and rub it in. Leave the mix on your scalp for around an hour before shampooing your hair with lukewarm water and then rinsing. You can repeat this procedure four or five times a month to help eliminate dandruff.

Rinsing your hair with a warm water solution with apple cider vinegar added can help alleviate dandruff. Try a 50:50 solution for an overall 'rinse', or treat a problem area by applying a tablespoon of apple cider vinegar onto the hair and massage gently with your fingertips. Wait a few minutes, then wash as normal and rinse well in warm water. The acetic acid in the vinegar kills the fungus *Malassezia furfur* and restores the pH balance of the scalp.

Remember that too-hot water will make the texture of your hair 'dry' while rubbing your scalp too much will stimulate the sebaceous glands to release their oils, resulting in greasy hair.

Reduce Hair Loss

Hair loss can be tackled by using a combination of lemon juice and coconut milk. Mix the juice of one lemon to 4 tbsp of coconut milk. Apply the mixture to the scalp at least once a week. Rinse your hair with warm water to remove the mixture and then shampoo and condition as normal.

Scalp Treatment

This is an effective hair and scalp treatment for all hair types. Combine an egg with 2 tbsp of honey, 2 tbsp of olive oil, 1 tbsp of lemon juice and a drop of two or your favorite essential oil. Mix everything together in a bowl and apply the mix over the hair and scalp. Leave for at least 20 minutes (but no longer than 40 minutes), then shampoo with lukewarm water. Finally give your hair and scalp a cold-water rinse. You can substitute the olive oil for sesame, coconut or almond oil if you wish.

Natural Hairspray

A great lemony hairspray, which works for all types of hair, is very simple to make. Slice four lemons and put them into a saucepan with 900 ml/1½ pints/3¾ cups of water. Simmer the mixture for 15 minutes, or until around half the water has evaporated. Then strain the liquid into a spray bottle and add a few drops of your favorite essential oil. Keep the spray bottle in the refrigerator and it should last for at least a week.

Shiny Nails

To get lovely shiny nails, soak your fingernails (or toenails) in lemon juice for 10 minutes, and brush them with a toothbrush or a small nail brush using a mixture of white wine vinegar and warm water (2 tbsp each), mixed with the juice of half a lemon. It will help your nails stay bright, strong and shiny. This is also a good way of removing the yellow color that develops with the regular use of nail polish.

Smoking and using nail polish can lead to discolored nails. Simply cut a fresh lemon and squeeze the juice into a shallow bowl. Soak your nails and fingertips in the lemon juice for several minutes. Repeat this over a number of days to rid your nails of any yellowing. After each treatment wash and rinse your hands and apply a moisturizer.

Strong Nails

To soften your cuticles and strengthen your nails at the same time add 3 tbsp of freshly squeezed lemon juice to a little liquid soap. Add a few drops of warm water and soak your nails in this mixture for five minutes. This will leave your fingers feeling soft and your nails strong and healthy looking.

If you have brittle fingernails, try rubbing sliced lemon every day on them. This will help your nails become much stronger and sturdier.

Soften Cuticles

A manicure or pedicure requires attention not only to the nails but to the cuticles as well. Soften cuticles by soaking your fingers and toes in white vinegar for 5 minutes.

Longer Lasting Nail Polish

Nail polish lasts longer if you dampen the nails first with a cotton wool ball soaked in apple cider or white vinegar. Let the nails dry briefly then apply your favorite shade.

Healthy Toenails

While you are pampering your feet, take a moment or two to inspect the condition of your toenails: modern synthetic hosiery, training shoes and wearing closed shoes for days on end where toes are in slightly damp, dark and airless conditions can provide the ideal home for fungal infections which often go unnoticed until they become a real problem.

Give foot fungus the boot with regular footbaths made of 1 part vinegar to 2 parts warm water. Sit back, relax and soak away aching feet safe in the knowledge that they will be deodorized, softened and healthy – perfect for going shoe shopping!

Teeth & Mouth

Whitening Teeth and Stain Removal

We all know that some of the proprietary brands of whitening toothpastes contain baking soda. But you can use a little baking soda once a week on your wet toothbrush to do much the same thing. Just dip your wet toothbrush into a little baking soda and brush your teeth as normal. The baking soda also helps remove any stubborn stains from your teeth. You should not swallow this paste and only use it if there are no signs of rawness on your gums.

For badly stained teeth you could add a little hydrogen peroxide, although this should be used with care and definitely not swallowed.

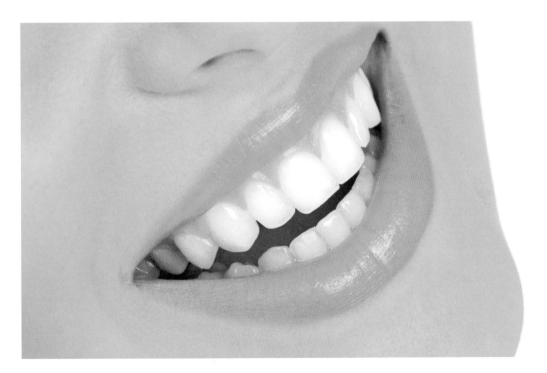

Bespoke Toothpaste

If you like the taste of your regular toothpaste then why not add some baking soda to it? By mixing the two together and placing the mixture into a sealed container, the mix will keep for ages. It will help keep down the plaque, as well as the stains, and keep your teeth whiter at the same time.

Cleaning on the Move

Wherever you are, if you are expecting to get close or speak to people, it is always nice to feel confident that your mouth is fresh. If you are off to a meeting or a hot date then dipping a piece of chewing gum into water and then into a small amount of baking soda can really help to make your mouth feel fresh and clean. Might be worth keeping a phial of it in your handbag or in the glove compartment of your car, just in case?

Plaque Removal

We all know how quickly plaque and tartar build up on the teeth and how much better the teeth feel when the dentist has cleaned them. Using baking soda mixed with iodized salt on a wet toothbrush can help keep the plaque down.

Cleaning Toothbrushes

We all do it – we grab the toothbrush without really giving any thought to the germs or bacteria that might be hiding on it. But the toothbrush can retain any number of germs and bacteria. To kill them you can soak your toothbrush in a weak paste made of baking soda and water mixed together. The toothbrush would be fine soaking all night and at least you would have peace of mind that it is clean when you come to use it the next morning.

Breath Freshener

You can make your own breath freshener – particularly useful if you dined on onions or garlic the night before! Using a gargle made of ½ teaspoon baking soda mixed with water could be part of your daily routine. This mix can kill off any germs and leave your mouth feeling much fresher.

When you really feel as if you should hide away from the world because of lingering breath odor, use ⅛ teaspoon baking soda mixed with water as an instant breath freshener. Swish it around like a mouthwash and it will neutralize the lingering bad odors.

Retainers and Dentures

Braces, retainers and dentures can be soaked overnight in a mixture of baking soda and water. This mixture helps to kill off any germs that might have accumulated. It also helps to keep retainers looking bright and shiny.

If dentures are badly stained they can be scrubbed with a toothbrush that has been dipped in a baking soda paste.

Odor & Feet

Underarm Deodorant

You can even use baking soda to make an underarm deodorant – how cool is that? Just mix together 4 teaspoons potassium alum (which you can buy in block form; it is used as an aftershave and rubbed over a freshly shaven face) with 2 teaspoons baking soda and 250 ml/8 fl oz/1 cup alcohol. You can decant the mixture into a suitable plastic spray-capped bottle and it can be used daily. It keeps you fresh and dry all day long and the added bonus is that it does not contain any harmful chemicals.

The antibacterial and deodorizing properties of vinegar can be harnessed by splashing or dabbing a little white vinegar under each arm. You can even steep a few leaves of herbs – sage is good – in the vinegar if you want a 'scented' lotion (sage is also 'cooling' on the skin). As well as combating odor, the vinegar will not make those white marks on your clothes that many ordinary antiperspirants leave behind.

In an emergency, lemons can be used as a short-term deodorizer. Either dab a little lemon extract to freshen up your armpits, or rub a wedge of lemon onto the skin of the armpit. It will only last for a few hours, but it is effective.

CAUTION: Do not apply lemon or vinegar to broken skin (or after hair removal by shaving) as it will sting!

Body Odor

Adding 100 g/ 4 oz/½ cup baking soda to the bath water will help eliminate perspiration smells, as well as neutralizing acids and dispersing oil. If you use baking soda like a talcum powder and apply it to your body with a powder puff then you will feel fresh all day long. You can use it all over to keep the odors at bay.

Hands

You have just finished preparing a beautiful meal and the guests are due to arrive. You put your hands to your face, only to discover that they smell of garlic, onion and any combination of different food smells. Don't worry though; a little baking soda used as soap with a little water will quickly neutralize the smells and make you feel much better.

If your hands are particularly dirty, you can mix one measure of baking soda with three parts of either water or liquid hand wash to clean them up, then rinse off the grime. And don't forget to add some baking soda to the dishwashing water, too.

Talcum Powder

Baking soda straight from the pack works just like a talcum powder if you sprinkle it on to your skin. The baking soda helps absorb any excess moisture, particularly when the temperature is high, it is a bit too humid and you've been perspiring. Just like your favorite talcum powder, the baking soda makes you feel fresh all-over.

Smelly Feet

Smelly or itchy feet can really plague some people in the hot weather. But using baking soda as a talcum powder first thing in the morning can help keep the feet dry and itch-free all day. Use it before you put on your socks and footwear. Good for your feet and good for those around them too!

Tired Feet

If you've been on your feet all day at work, or spent the day 'shopping till you nearly dropped' then a foot bath can feel wonderful. If you mix 200 g/7 oz/1 cup baking soda into some comfortably hot water, lower your feet gently in and then relax, you'll be amazed how wonderful your feet feel afterwards. And your feet get softened too!

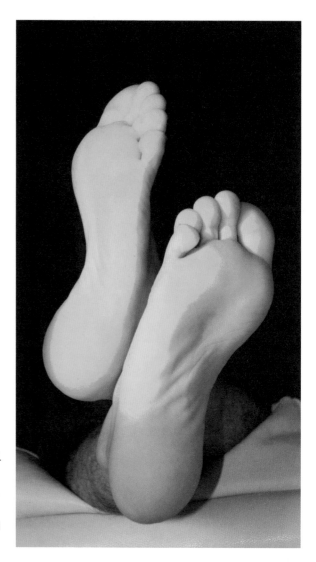

Apple Cider Vinegar

'An apple a day keeps the doctor away.'

This old rhyme does contain a great deal of truth: like many fruits, apples contain vitamins, minerals and other antioxidant properties which may help to reduce the risk of cancer by preventing DNA damage. Boron, the mineral that is found in apples, may retard bone loss in women after menopause and possibly help women on estrogen replacement therapy keep the estrogen in their blood stream for longer.

A Multipurpose Natural Remedy

In recent years apple cider vinegar has become one of the most popular 'natural remedies' for a whole range of ailments. There have been scientific studies and medical trials supporting some of this vinegar's benefits in our diet: it can reduce cholesterol and 2 tablespoons (30 ml/⅛ cup) added to our diet has been shown to reduce the GI (glycemic index) of carbohydrate food. Potassium, which is found in apple cider vinegar, is vital to good health: a potassium deficiency can cause a variety of conditions including hair loss, brittle nails and sinusitis.

Vinegar also contains malic acid, which has been found to destroy micro-organisms including fungi and bacteria – which is why it has for thousands of years been used for pickling and preserving foods. Scientists

now know that vinegar also inhibits the growth of gram-negative bacilli (the most well known of which are the bacteria *E. Coli* and *Salmonella*) and because it balances the acid levels in the body, vinegar can help keep the levels of gut flora such as *Candida albicans* in the digestive tract at healthy levels: low acid levels can encourage the growth of fungal infections such as *candidiasis* (also known as 'thrush').

A Reliable Remedy?

Many of the claims for vinegar's curative properties, including 'miraculous weight-loss vinegar diets' and 'cures' for arthritis (involving drinking a mix of honey, apple cider vinegar, water and kelp three times a day) remain untested and unproven, but incredibly popular nonetheless and with a great deal of anecdotal support. Many advocates of apple-cider-vinegar 'cures' claim the acidic content of apple cider vinegar 'breaks down fat', supposedly leading to weight loss, and that the malic acid dissolves uric acid deposits that can form around joints and cause swelling and pain.

Most champions of 'vinegar treatments' recommend apple cider vinegar, but to be truly effective this must be made from fresh, organic, crushed apples that are allowed to mature naturally in wooden barrels. Such 'raw' or 'natural' apple cider vinegar can be found in most good health food shops and should have the vinegar mother clearly present as sediment in the bottom of the bottle. Distilling or pasteurizing apple cider vinegar will have removed not only the vinegar mother, but destroyed many minerals and trace elements including potassium, phosphorus, sulphur, magnesium, iron and copper. Also destroyed in pasteurization are malic and tartaric acids that may be beneficial in fighting toxins and inhibiting bacterial, yeast and fungal growth in the intestinal tract.

Some Drawbacks

While there are no long-term side effects to ingesting apple cider vinegar in moderation, the big drawbacks to drinking substantially larger quantities of vinegar than what you would eat in the form of salad dressing are the strong taste and the potential deterioration of dental enamel. This can give your teeth a yellowish appearance and make them much more sensitive to heat and cold. Some suggest apple cider vinegar is made more palatable by mixing it with apple juice, or with baking soda which neutralizes the acid to between 6.0 and 7.0 pH.

Be Prepared

If you are going to try apple cider vinegar for remedial purposes, it is also recommended that you carry out an investigation of your own by buying a pH-testing kit (you can purchase these at a local pharmacies). You can test your urine to see if you are more alkaline or acid so that you can adjust the amount of apple cider vinegar doses. You should also start with a thorough, in-depth investigation of the literature available in books and online, in tandem with a consultation with your medical practitioner.

The majority of the remedies that use vinegar in the following section use apple cider vinegar (or in some instances white vinegar) as external applications: the nearest any vinegar will get to your mouth is in the form of a mouth wash, and like any other mouthwash, you spit it out after gargling! If you are going to 'eat' vinegar, then it should be a pleasure – as part of a delicious and nutritious meal.

CAUTION: Do not attempt self-diagnosis or self-treatment: always seek qualified advice for any medical condition.

Natural Remedies

As we have seen, apple cider vinegar has recently been 'rediscovered' and found to be effective in offering relief from a range of symptoms of common illnesses and infections. But it is not just apples that are good for us. Lemons can be used for a whole range of health conditions. Meanwhile, baking soda is so safe to use that you can also ingest it. Although it is artificially produced for mass use, it is a compound that also occurs naturally as sedimentary mineral deposits. That's why it is so good to use as a healthcare product.

Head & Face

Sore and Puffy Eyes

Of course it is never advisable to put neat lemon juice into the eyes, but adding a drop or two of lemon juice to a cup of warm water will do you no harm. Simply use the solution as you would a normal eye wash to soothe sore eyes.

If your eyes are a bit puffy, maybe from hay fever or a particularly late night, try squeezing the juice of a lemon into a small bowl. Add two slices of cucumber to the lemon juice and let the slices sit in the juice for a minute or two. Place one of the cucumber slices over each eye and relax. This will not only get rid of puffy eyes, but will also help to reduce dark circles underneath the eyes.

Itchy Eyes

If you are suffering from itchy eyes, which could be the result of an allergy to pollen, you can soothe them with baking soda eyewash. Add ½ teaspoon baking soda to half a glass of water and bathe the eyes with an eyebath. The mixture will keep in the fridge for a couple of days.

Contact Lenses

Daily wear contact lenses need cleaning every day. Add a pinch of baking soda to your cleaner to make it mildly abrasive. This helps prevent build-up and could extend the life of the lenses.

Chapped Lips

Chapped lips can sting and make you feel very miserable in the winter months. Place a small amount of Vaseline or glycerine onto a saucer and mix in the juice of half a lemon. Apply your homemade lip balm to your lips to heal and soothe.

Cold Sores

Cold sores are caused by a viral infection (known as herpes simplex type 1) and are small, painful fluid-filled blisters on the mouth or round the nostrils. Once you have had a cold sore, the virus lies dormant in the nerves or skin around the original site until something – a cold, the flu, stress or generally being 'run down' – causes another outbreak. You can treat a cold sore with some baking soda mixed with a little water. Gently – and we mean gently – rub the sore. You will feel relief and it will speed up the healing process. The cold sore virus can be carried on your toothbrush, so remember to soak that in baking soda too.

You can sooth the pain and swelling, and perhaps 'disinfect' the sore by dabbing with a cotton wool ball soaked in apple cider vinegar three times a day.

Lemons have been used to deal with cold sores for generations. Simply cut a slice of lemon and place it directly onto the affected spot. It will sting, but try to keep it there for as long as you can bear it. Change the slice and reapply. To help avoid cold sores from developing, try squeezing four lemons into a glass of water for a daily drink. This will give your body an extra boost that will both prevent and treat cold sores.

CAUTION: Only apply the lemon slice treatment at the beginning of a cold sore outbreak. Do not use on open sores or broken skin.

Gum Disease and Other Mouth Problems

You will need to brace yourself for this because it involves chewing the peel of a lemon! The natural healing properties of lemons will act on your gums and strengthen them, as well as killing off and inhibiting mouth bacteria, which can cause gum disease.

Fresh lemon juice can also be applied if you have a toothache. The sharp, tangy liquid will help reduce the pain.

If you massage lemon juice onto bleeding gums it will help stop the bleeding.

Earache

For an effective remedy for earache, squeeze a little lemon juice and add to a similar amount of mustard oil. Heat the two fluids together until you have an oily residue. When you have earache put a couple of drops into the ear and this will help ease the pain.

Nose Bleeds

The lemon's peel, pith and core can help strengthen blood vessels and lemon juice has strong astringent properties. If you have a nose bleed, soak a cotton wool ball in lemon juice and put the ball into the affected nostril. Leave the cotton wool ball in your nostril for at least 10 minutes. The lemon juice will help to seal the broken blood vessels by tightening up the membranes in your nose.

Nitty-Gritty

Head lice, known scientifically as Pediculosis capitis are commonly associated with school children, but adults can get them too. Contrary to popular opinion which implies that those who get head lice have dirty hair, head lice adore squeaky clean and preferably fine, straight hair. The lice are keen travellers looking for 'human hotels' and are most often spread by being transferred between clothing.

While head lice themselves do not transmit disease, unless treated, their itchy infestation can be embarrassing and make life a misery. The wingless 1-mm lice feed on the scalp and lay their eggs – the nits – which are each 'glued' to a single hair close to the scalp.

An over-the-counter preparation will kill the lice, but after shampooing, an extra treatment rinsing an infected head with white vinegar will dissolve the 'glue' holding the eggs to the hair which should then be combed out using a very fine-toothed comb. The treatment will need to be repeated every 4–5 days until the hair is clear of infestation.

The horror of head lice can be averted in the first place by simply adding two drops of lemon oil into your shampoo. Then add another two drops into your hair conditioner. The presence of the acidic lemon will help to deter the outbreak of an infestation of head lice or make life uncomfortable for them if they have already arrived.

Hands & Feet

Dry Hands

If you have dry hands, simply squeeze the juice of a lemon into a bowl of warm water. Dunk your hands into the soothing mixture. Keep your hands immersed for two or three minutes, then dry them off and pour a little olive oil into the palm of your hand. Gently rub in the olive oil, massaging it into your hands.

Fingertip Splits

Fingertip splits can really hurt. Lemon oil can not only speed their healing, but will also soften the skin and soothe. All you need to do is to bury your finger tip in a piece of lemon peel. This will release the oil in the lemon, which will soak into the split skin wound. Repeat the process two or three times a day until the split is healed.

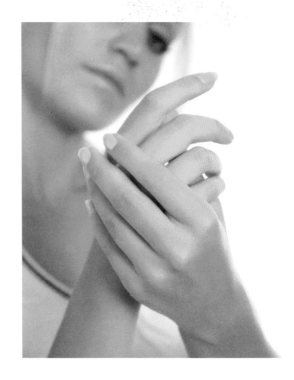

Chilblains

Chilblains are caused by fluid leaking out of tiny blood vessels into your skin. Lemons can help reduce the swelling and the itchy sensation. All you need to do is make sure that you include lemon juice and zest in your everyday diet.

Soothe Sore, Aching Feet

After an exhausting days' shopping, your feet might be grateful for the soothing and healing properties of a lemon. If your feet are sore, rub a sliced lemon over the burning part of the foot to relieve the pain and eliminate any toxins.

Make yourself a wonderful foot soak by squeezing the juice of a lemon into a bowl of warm water. This will help to cool the feet and promote a good nights' sleep by relaxing the throbbing. After soaking the feet, massage them with olive oil. This also works if your hands are extremely dry.

Swollen Ankles

There can be many reasons why your ankles might swell; there could be an underlying problem that results in fluid retention, so of course it is always best to consult your doctor if this is a persistent problem.

However, lemons can help strengthen the walls of veins and they are also a diuretic, which encourages the production of urine. This will help reduce fluid retention. To help prevent swollen ankles, include lemons, particularly the juice and zest, in your daily diet.

Athlete's Foot

Medically known as Tinea pedis, you do not have to be an athlete to suffer from this fungal infection. It commonly affects the feet but it can be spread – on bath towels – to other parts of the body (especially the crotch) because the fungus needs a nice warm, moist and dark place to thrive!

Keeping feet (and other 'bits') dry, and going barefoot whenever possible, are recommended, but to get rid of the fungus itself (and ease the itching) rinse your feet three or four times a day with undiluted apple cider vinegar.

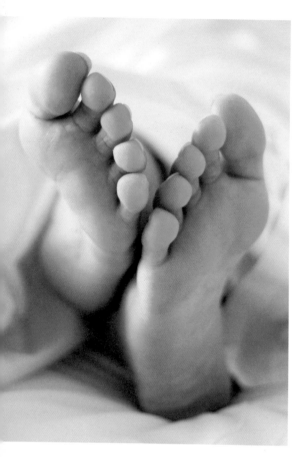

To guard against re-infection, soak your socks (and jocks!) in a solution of 1 part white vinegar and 4 parts warm water for 30 minutes before laundering them.

Lemon juice can help too. Soak a cotton wool ball in lemon juice and apply directly to the infected area, or squeeze the juice of a lemon into a bowl of warm water or foot bath and bathe your feet in it for ten minutes.

Corns and Calluses

Corns are hard little 'mountains' formed by increased growth of the skin on toes and are often caused by wearing shoes that are too tight. Calluses are areas of skin that have become toughened through repeated contact or pressure and are most common on the hands.

A traditional remedy for both these problems is to saturate a slice of stale white bread in white vinegar and let it soak for 30 minutes. Then break off a piece of bread large enough to cover the corn or callused area. Keep the poultice in place with a gauze bandage and leave it on overnight.

The next morning the callused skin should have 'dissolved' and a corn should be easier to remove. Older, harder corns and calluses may need a few treatments.

Lemons are also good for dealing with corns and calluses. You can either apply neat lemon juice directly three times a day, or you can use lemon oil as an accelerating process. The overnight alternative is to place either a slice of lemon or the peel of a lemon onto the corn and stick it in place with a plaster.

CAUTION: When applying lemon oil always make sure that the undiluted oil is only applied to the corn or callus, as it could damage normal skin.

Skin & Body

Soothe Allergic Skin

If you are allergic to anything at all, from food to medication, more often than not the symptoms will show up on the skin in the form of a rash. These skin allergies can often take the shape of unsightly hives, which are very itchy and take ages to disappear. Although baking soda cannot help with curing the allergy, using it in your bath water can bring enormous relief from the itching. Using 400 g/14 oz/2 cups in a cool bath should be enough to relieve the symptoms, but if you find that particular areas of the body are causing you more intense discomfort, then neat baking soda can be rubbed into these areas for even more relief.

Psoriasis

The citric acid in lemon juice should help ease flaky and dry skin and also help deal with the underlying inflammation caused by psoriasis. As an anti-inflammatory, applying neat lemon juice to psoriasis patches several times a day and then exposing those patches to direct sunlight for a few minutes will help. This is a home-cure version of a similar treatment used by dermatologists. Those with psoriasis should certainly incorporate lemons into their regular daily diet, too.

Eczema

Eczema is a very irritating skin condition. You can create a lemon wrap to relieve your skin from this itching by either squeezing the juice of a whole lemon or four drops of lemon oil into 250 ml/8 fl oz/1 cup of warm water and 1 tbsp of honey. Soak a clean cloth in the liquid and squeeze out the excess. Place the cloth over the affected area and leave it there for 15 minutes.

You can repeat this process two or three times a day. This brilliant mixture will not only ease any infection but it will stop you from wanting to scratch. The lemon will heal and the honey acts as an anti-inflammatory, too. Another way to relieve itchy skin is to squeeze the juice of two lemons into a warm bath and have a soak.

CAUTION: Eczema can cause broken skin often due to scratching, which may be aggravated by lemon juice. Also, people with sensitive skin, who are prone to conditions such as eczema and psoriasis, are often allergic or intolerant to citrus fruits. Anyone with a strong and persistent problem with eczema and psoriasis should consult their dermatologist or doctor before using any of these lemon-based treatments.

Poison Ivy

Poison ivy can give you a dreadful rash. The traditional treatment is to use camomile lotion, but lemons are quicker, easier to obtain and more effective.

Squeeze the juice of a lemon into a bowl. Dunk a cotton wool pad into the juice and apply it directly to the rash area to reduce the inflammation and soothe the itching sensation.

Alternatively, soak in a bath containing 100 g/4 oz/½ cup baking soda.

Generally Itchy Skin

The temptation when you get an itch is to scratch, and so break the skin. Insect bites are a common cause of itchiness but a paste made from vinegar and cornstarch will help reduce the urge to scratch.

For overall dry and itchy skin, 2 tablespoons vinegar added to your bath water will help soothe the itch and, being more relaxed, it should also make you less 'antsy'.

Anti-Aging

Lemons are a wonderful source of Vitamin C. This vitamin encourages the body to make collagen, which is used to build joints, bones, ligaments and blood vessels. By ensuring that lemons are part of your daily diet your body will be more able to repair muscles and keep them healthy, as well as giving your skin every chance to stay fresh and youthful.

Cellulite

Lemon juice is ideal for a wide range of skin problems. Cellulite is a dimpling of the skin where there is excess tissue fluid. Massage lemon oil onto the affected area. As lemons are rich in Vitamin C and also act as a diuretic, you can either make sure that you include lemon juice and zest in your daily diet, or add two drops of lemon oil to your bath water and rub the dimpled skin area with a loofah. Using lemon juice in this way should reduce excess tissue fluid and therefore cellulite marks.

Broken Veins

Lemon juice or lemon oil is very effective for treating circulatory problems, such as broken capillaries, or spider veins. Lemons contain Vitamin P in the peel and the juice, so lemons are great for keeping your capillaries strong and strengthening the arterial system. For spider veins add two or three drops of lemon oil to jojoba or almond oil and massage into the affected area.

Varicose Veins

The natural astringent and anti-inflammatory qualities of the lemon will strengthen the walls of veins. To help reduce the appearance of varicose veins, mix two drops of lemon oil with three drops of cypress oil and two drops of lavender oil, along with 2 tbsp of almond oil. Massage the mixture directly onto the area affected by the varicose veins. Repeat the treatment once a day until you begin to see results.

Alternatively, try this for relief: soak some 'bandages' made from clean cotton fabric in vinegar and wrap them around your legs – not too tightly – and lie down for 30 minutes with your legs comfortably supported so your feet are above the level of your head.

Wart Removal

If you are prone to warts, a preventative measure is to drink the juice of a whole lemon each day. You can, of course, water this down, and perhaps add a dash of sugar to make it more palatable.

For generations people have thought that rubbing a potato onto a wart and then burying the potato is a sure-fire wart cure. What certainly does work is rubbing lemon juice directly onto the wart and covering it with a plaster. Repeat the procedure every day for at least two weeks. Slowly but surely the lemon juice will dissolve the wart.

Bruises

Lemon peel and lemon juice can actually limit bruising and also speed the recovery from a bruise. Either rub lemon peel onto the affected area, or include the juice of a lemon and its zest in your regular diet.

Burn Marks

Burns are painful and can cause swelling, redness or even blisters. If you burn your hand on the oven, or touch the iron, turn to lemon juice for the solution. All you will need is lemon juice, tomato extract and almond oil.

Rinse the burn under cool, running water and cover the mark with a dampened cloth. Then dampen the cloth with lemon juice and apply it to the burn. This will help to cleanse the skin and lighten the burn mark. Repeat this treatment to thoroughly cleanse the area before rubbing tomato extract onto the burn mark. The tomato will naturally bleach the area. To complete the recovery process, apply some almond oil to soften the skin, improve the skin color and remove what is left of the burn mark. This treatment should not only help to heal the burn, but also accelerate the skin lightening process. You can use the pulp of a tomato instead of tomato extract and coconut oil instead of almond oil if you prefer.

Ease Sunburn and Windburn

In much the same way as baking soda brings relief from allergic skin reactions, 400 g/14 oz/2 cups of baking soda can also be added to a cool bath if you are suffering from sunburn or have been out in a strong wind for too long. It will help take the burn out of the skin, but obviously cannot remedy any other symptoms of too much sun that you might be suffering. If you've been on a boat and got windburn on your face the baking soda will soon soothe your skin.

As lemon juice is such an efficient astringent, its healing properties will help calm irritated, sunburned skin. Squeeze the juice of a lemon into a bowl and add three times the amount of water. Apply this gently and directly onto the sunburned skin using a cotton wool pad.

If you have badly burned your skin, then add three drops of lemon oil to 2 tbsp of almond oil and apply this to the sunburned area.

Try vinegar too: cool sunburn by gently dabbing the affected area with a cotton ball or a soft cloth saturated with white or cider vinegar. This treatment is most effective if you can treat the burn before it starts to sting.

Deal with Chickenpox Spots

If you cast your mind back to when you were a child and had those awful childhood illnesses, you may well remember how uncomfortable chickenpox was. There was the constant itching and the constant rebukes from your parents that you would scar yourself if you scratched the spots. Well, if you ever come into contact with some poor soul who is suffering from similar problems, suggest that they make a paste of baking soda and a little cool water. This can be applied directly to the spots without any fear of additional irritation. The paste will soothe the itching and make the patient feel much more comfortable.

Relieve Insect Bites and Stings

How annoying is it when those nasty little bugs creep up on you and give you such a bite that you feel as if a lion has mauled you? The worst ones are those mosquitoes, which you can only hear and not see. These insect bites, or stings from wasps, are so itchy that sometimes you cannot sleep for wanting to scratch. And you know it is best not to touch them. If you mix some baking soda into a paste with a little water and then smear it over the bite or sting, you will be amazed at how quickly it gives you relief from the itching.

Lemon juice will not only reduce the itching caused by insect bites, but it will also bring down any swelling. If you have been bitten by a cloud of mosquitoes, squeeze the juice of two lemons into a warm bath and bathe in it to reduce the itching and subsequent swelling. For other stings and bites, such as from a wasp, apply neat lemon juice with a cotton wool pad directly onto the bite site. Repeat this as often as necessary to bring down the inflammation and swelling. Lemon juice mixed with eucalyptus oil is also believed to be a great mosquito repellent.

You can alleviate the itch of mosquito bites and wasp stings in the same way with apple cider vinegar too. Not only will it calm the itch, but many claim that the scent of vinegar keeps the mosquitoes from coming back for a second helping.

CAUTION: If you have any redness and/or swelling 24 hours after being stung, you may have an infection, so consult a doctor. If you have had a severe reaction to a sting or bite in the past, you should consult your doctor about the need for an emergency syringe of epinephrine to be carried at all times outdoors.

Cuts and Grazes

Lemons are great antiseptics. The juice alone will deal with most minor cuts and grazes. They are also excellent for mouth ulcers. If you have a larger cut, rub either lemon peel or juice into the affected area. This will sting, but on the upside it will kill any infection and help soothe the inflammation.

Scars

Lemon and cucumber juice can be combined to help remove scarring, or at least to reduce the impact of a visible scar. Squeeze the juice of a lemon into a bowl and then add an equal amount of cucumber juice (to obtain the cucumber juice, grate the cucumber and then squeeze the juice from the pulp by wringing it in a dish towel) into the same bowl and mix. Gently dab the mixture onto the scarred tissue. Leave it to dry for up to 10 minutes, then wash off with water and pat dry. Repeat the treatment on a daily basis until the scar begins to fade.

CAUTION: Do not apply to freshly scarred areas or those that still have stitches in them.

Wart Remover

Warts are caused by a viral infection, specifically by the human papillomavirus. One folk remedy is to soak the wart for 20 minutes each day in white vinegar, followed by a gentle rub with an emery board, until it disappears. You could also apply a vinegar-soaked cotton pad and bandage this to the wart.

Sore Muscles

After a workout in the gym, a day of gardening or a long day's work, treat your aching muscles to a soak in a pleasantly hot tub with 120 ml/4 fl oz/½ cup of cider vinegar added to the bath water.

Internal Health

CAUTION: It is important to remember that all uses of lemons, vinegar and even baking soda on the body, especially internally and for serious conditions, should be practiced with caution and do not replace the advice of a doctor.

Anemia

If you are iron deficient then you may have a low level of stomach acid. The acidity in a lemon can help by lowering the pH level in your stomach. The pectin in a lemon is broken down by bacteria in the stomach, which creates fatty acids, which help us to boost iron absorption, which in turn helps to reduce anemia. Simply drink a glass of water containing a squeeze of lemon juice before each meal.

High Blood Pressure

Lemons can be very useful in helping tackle the causes and results of high blood pressure (hypertension). Lemons contain potassium and magnesium and they also promote healthy arteries, while their acids discourage insulin resistance.

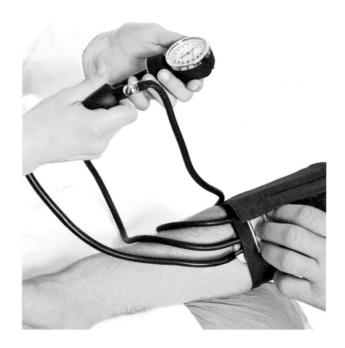

Just the flavor of a lemon discourages you from adding salt to your food. Salt is often associated with high blood pressure and should be used to a minimum.

Lemon juice also helps release calcium from meat and fish bones, which is valuable in ensuring stable blood-pressure levels.

To be even more scientific, lemon juice operates rather like an ace inhibitor. This simply means it helps decrease the production of a hormone called angiotensin, which has been shown to raise blood pressure by constricting blood vessels.

For generations Russians have used lemons to control blood pressure, and tests in Japan have shown that the consumption of lemon juice has been linked with a reduction in the number of patients with high blood pressure.

High Cholesterol

There are many reasons why you might have high cholesterol, such as insufficient sunlight or exercise or a poor diet. The liver creates most of the body's cholesterol and the lemon can have an impact on how this occurs.

The pectin in a lemon helps to reduce the absorption of cholesterol from food. In the gut pectin also helps inhibit cholesterol absorption. This, together with its Vitamin C, means that the lemon can deliver a double blow against cholesterol.

A lemon is often described as being an alkaline-forming food and research has shown that it does help dissolve and eliminate cholesterol. If you were to eat four apples every day then in terms of cholesterol lowering they would perform the same as a strong statin drug, which is designed to reduce cholesterol. Well, step aside apples, because lemons have more pectin in them, so they are even more effective!

Stuffy Nose and Chest Congestion

All bunged up? Using baking soda in a vaporizer can really help to clear a stuffy nose quickly. Fill the vaporizer with water to the indicated level then add and stir in 1 teaspoon salt and 1 teaspoon baking soda until they are dissolved. Now breathe in the vapor to clear the congestion. This is a really good tip for those who cannot or do not wish to use proprietary decongestants. Pregnant women, children and those who have medical conditions are often prevented from using medication. Baking soda is a safe alternative for everyone, whatever their circumstances.

Not only does baking soda in your vaporizer help clear your stuffy nose and reduce the symptoms of a cold, but it also deodorizes your house and removes lingering odors. How's that for good value!

Alternatively try vinegar: put 120 ml/4 fl oz/½ cup white vinegar into a heatproof bowl and pour on some boiling water. Breath in the steam-vapor. A towel over your head to keep the steam 'focused' will help.

Tight Chests

An old folk remedy for chest pains and 'aching ribs' caused by a cold, flu or by coughing is to soak a piece of brown paper in apple cider vinegar, then sprinkle one side of the wet paper liberally with pepper. Place the paper pepper side down against your chest and leave it there for 20–25 minutes.

Coughs

The oil in lemons can help expel mucus, so to soothe a cough you could make your own homemade lemonade (*see* page 235) and drink it daily.

Alternatively, slice half a lemon and use a pestle and mortar to break up 2 tbsp of linseeds. Put these into 600 ml/1 pint/2½ cups of water and simmer in a pan for 20 minutes. Strain and add honey to sweeten the mixture.

Another option is to boil up a bowl of water and add two drops each of lemon oil, eucalyptus oil and tea-tree oil. Put a towel over your head and inhale.

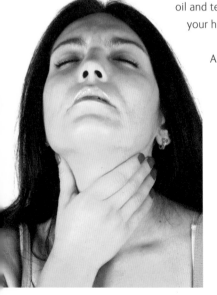

A further homemade cough remedy is to heat 4 tbsp of lemon juice, 180 ml/6 fl oz/scant ¾ cup of honey and 6 tbsp of olive oil. Stir the mixture while heating. Allow it to cool and then take 1 tsp of the mixture every two or three hours for the next 48 hours.

Sore Throat

Gargling is the solution for a sore throat. You will need to squeeze the juice of one lemon into a small amount of hot water. If you gargle three times a day with this mixture the soreness will subside as the lemon juice gets to work on the damaged areas of your throat and tackles the inflammation.

Fever Reduction

If one of your loved ones has a high fever there's nothing quite as effective and speedy to reduce the temperature as a baking soda bath. Add some baking soda to a cool, but not cold, bath and the temperature will plummet fast.

Children's high temperatures will really drop quickly if you pop them into the cool baking soda bath. They will feel much more comfortable. Of course the added bonus is that it washes them squeaky clean at the same time as lowering their temperature.

Immune System Strengthening

The Vitamin C in a lemon is great for improving your overall immunity. Pectin fiber in the lemons stimulates the production of antibodies and white blood cells. They also help create a protein, which deals with inflammation. So making sure that lemons are in your daily diet can certainly help your overall immunity to fight off coughs, colds, infections or viruses.

Anti-Inflammatory

The lemon can work as a wonderful anti-inflammatory. Squeeze half a fresh lemon into a glass and add 1 tsp of agave (a natural sweetener from Mexico or South Africa). Alternatively, add 10 drops of stevia, another sweetener and part of the sunflower family. Add a tiny amount of turmeric to taste and top up the glass with spring water. Drink this anti-inflammatory internal cleanser every two hours and drink plenty of water in between each dose.

Arthritis

As lemons are anti-inflammatory, the antioxidant properties of a lemon's peel and juice can help with most types of arthritis. Grate the peel of a lemon and rub this over the aching joint. Make sure that you do not apply the pith. Wrap the joint after applying the lemon peel with a bandage and leave it for at least two hours.

Alternatively, squeeze half a lemon into a small amount of almond oil and massage the painful joint.

It is also possible to relieve painful joints by drinking the juice of a whole lemon in a glass of warm water each day.

Gout

Drinking the juice of a lemon in some warm water can help gout sufferers. Gout is caused by uric acid in the blood and tissue. This acid crystallizes in the joints, causing intense pain. The juice of a lemon can encourage the body to create calcium carbonate, which neutralizes uric acid.

Joint and Nerve Pain

Lemon juice has anti-inflammatory and cooling properties, so it is ideal for applying directly to troublesome joints and painful limbs, including areas that might be suffering from neuralgia. The simple solution is to warm the juice of a lemon and apply it directly to the affected area. Repeat the treatment each hour for at least half a day.

As an alternative you could try putting three drops of lemon oil into a little almond oil and using this as a massage oil for the affected area.

Neuralgia

Neuralgia can be very painful and once again the anti-inflammatory properties of the lemon can come to the rescue. Ideally you should use warm lemon juice, so pop a lemon into the microwave for 30 seconds, cut it in half and squeeze out the juice. This heating process will also encourage more juice to be released from the lemon. Rub the lemon juice onto the area affected by the neuralgia and repeat this as often as you need to reduce the pain.

Anxiety and Stress

If you are suffering from anxiety, the simplest and most irritating thing that people can tell you to do is to relax.

But it is good advice, and lemons can help. Bizarrely, the solution is to pour a cup of tea into a hot bath. The bath needs to be as hot as you can bear, but before clambering in, you need to put two lemon tea bags into a bowl. Half fill the bowl with hot water, add a dash of milk and then squeeze in the juice from a whole lemon. Pour this mixture into your bath and gently relax for at least 30 minutes.

Stress, which is often the cause of anxiety, can also be tackled by either improving your consumption of Vitamin C, or by using lemon oil to alleviate the symptoms. To increase your Vitamin C intake squeeze the juice of a lemon into a glass, top up with water and drink first thing daily. Alternatively, have a paper tissue handy and soak up a couple of drops of lemon oil. Inhale whenever you feel stress overtaking you.

Depression

Inhaling the vapor from lemon oil is believed by some psychologists to help ease depression. Simply put a few drops of lemon oil into a diffuser. Alternatively, if you do not have lemon oil readily available, put a few drops of lemon juice onto a paper tissue and inhale it from time to time.

Fainting and Fatigue

A lemon's acidity and fiber should slow down the absorption of sugar from the gut. This in turn helps prevent high blood sugar and then low blood sugar, which is often the cause of fainting.

Adding lemon juice and zest to your daily diet can help eliminate dizzy spells. Many people who use up their blood sugar quickly often feel faint after eating, so acidic foods help to promote the digestion of the food's proteins.

For fatigue, the fiber in a lemon helps to slow down sugar absorption. Lemons are packed with vitamins, and they contain some Vitamin B, which is good at alleviating fatigue. If you tend to get really tired make sure you are including some lemon juice and zest in your daily diet, too.

Insomnia

Relaxation and calming the brain are the keys to having a restful night's sleep. The simple solution is to drink lemon tea as your last beverage of the night.

Alternatively you can inhale the vapor from lemon oil, which is believed to have sedative properties. You can always drop some lemon oil into the bath before bedtime.

A slightly more complex way of dealing with insomnia is to mix a few drops of lemon oil, ylang ylang oil and vetivert oil together. The ylang ylang is believed to be an anti-depressant and the vetivert a comforting sedative. Massage your stomach with this oil mix before getting into bed. Some people also swear by putting a few drops of lemon oil onto their pillow.

You could also try mixing 2 tsp of lemon juice with 2 tbsp of honey and combining this in a cup of warm milk. Warming the milk activates the natural tryptophan the liquid contains and this induces sleep. Drink this warm, lemony milk drink about 30 minutes before bedtime.

Vitamin C Deficiency

The most extreme case of Vitamin C deficiency is one that used to afflict mariners in the past – scurvy. This presented itself as thinning hair, dry, flaky skin, fatigue and bleeding gums. The solution was to drink lemon or lime juice every day. Lemon juice is one of the best sources of Vitamin C.

Humans are one of the few animals that are unable to make their own Vitamin C, and the exact amount of Vitamin C that your body needs depends on your age and general health. Vitamin C is vital to help with cardiovascular and joint problems and cataracts, which are associated with Vitamin C deficiency. Vitamin C acts as an antioxidant and prevents oxygen-based damage to cells. Many of our cells are dependent on Vitamin C for protection. A deficiency will show itself if you become susceptible to colds and infections, as well as having a generally weak immune system. You may also become susceptible to respiratory infections and lung problems.

Lemon juice also has flavonoids, which are powerful antioxidants that fight the aging process and help us to fight disease.

Asthma

In addition to your inhaler, there are several ways in which lemon juice can be used to help ease asthma and prevent asthma attacks – the anti-inflammatory antioxidants in the lemon can come to the rescue if you have inflamed or sensitive airways.

Squeeze the juice of half a lemon and drink this with a little water two or three times a day. This will help prevent asthma attacks as it reduces the inflammation of the airway.

If you are suffering from an asthma attack, squeeze a little lemon juice into a glass of water and sip it over the course of the next 30 minutes. Wait for another 30 minutes and repeat.

Some asthma sufferers swear by pure lemon juice. They take half a spoonful before each meal and another before they go to bed.

Another option is to prepare a strong lemon solution. Squeeze the juice of a whole lemon into a cup and add boiling water and some honey to taste. Sip the drink while you inhale the steam.

Hay Fever

Lemons have anti-inflammatory and antihistamine properties, which can both help to discourage hay fever or allergic reactions. If you have hay fever you could try squeezing the juice of half a lemon into a glass of water. You should drink three of these lemony drinks during the course of the day. If the hay fever or allergy has given you a sore throat then gargle the mixture, but this time use warm water.

Bronchitis

Lemon juice is packed with Vitamin C and citric acid, so it is ideal for helping to deal with chest complaints such as bronchitis. When you have bronchitis it is best to drink plenty of fluids, as this helps get rid of the mucus. Lemon juice, particularly if taken with a little warm water, will also soothe an irritating cough.

To also aid your breathing, squeeze the juice of a lemon into a bowl of steaming hot water. Cover your head with a towel and breathe in the steam. For extra relief add a few drops of eucalyptus, peppermint or rosemary oil, as these will also help to clear your airways and soothe the irritation.

Hiccups

Medically known as singultis, hiccups are caused by a sudden spasm of the diaphragm which causes air to be rushed into the lungs, leading the epiglottis to close – which is the 'hic' sound in the hiccups.

A bout of hiccups normally resolves itself, but an old remedy that claims to 'cure' hiccups is a teaspoon of apple cider vinegar. Rather than any medicinal properties in the vinegar effecting a 'cure', it is more likely to be the sour taste – making your screw your face up and hold your breath – that does the trick!

Bad Breath

Lemons can be used as a mouthwash, as the juice is a great antiseptic. Squeeze the juice of a lemon into a glass and gargle with it. If you are feeling brave you can swallow the juice, or alternatively spit out and rinse the mouth. The citric acid kills off the bacteria in your mouth and alters the pH level of the body.

CAUTION: Do not gargle with lemon juice in your mouth for too long as it can affect the enamel on the teeth.

Hangovers

Hangovers can give you a headache, they can make you feel dehydrated and sometimes nauseous. For the headache you can rub a slice of lemon on your temple and forehead, or squeeze half a lemon into a cup of strong, black coffee. Alternatively, squeeze the juice of half a lemon onto a tissue and inhale.

For the hangover, and to give you a perk up, cut a lemon into quarter wedges and then sprinkle each quarter with salt. Brace yourself as you then eat the pulp, but not the pith or rind. This is guaranteed to wake you up!

Some people believe that prevention is far better than a cure. So if you have had a heavy night then squeeze the juice of a lemon into a glass of water and drink it before you go to bed. The Vitamin C in the lemon will help break down the alcohol in the liver. The lemon juice will also help with rehydration and your Vitamin C levels will be higher when you wake up in the morning.

Headaches

We've already seen that a headache brought on by a hangover can easily be dealt with using lemons. Whether you prefer tea or coffee first thing in the morning, if you have a regular headache just squeeze the juice of a lemon into your first cup.

An alternative for curing a headache with lemons is to sponge your head with the juice of half a lemon in a cup of water. It is also believed that inhaling the vapor from lemon juice can get rid of a headache.

Mouth Ulcers

This is going to sting! But there is no way of avoiding it if you want to get rid of that painful mouth ulcer.

Squeeze the juice of a lemon into a glass of water and gargle with it. The lemon juice will kill off bacteria and disinfect the ulcer. If you are feeling particularly brave there are two more treatments that will guarantee to make you wince.

The first is simple enough. Squeeze out some lemon juice, dip a cotton bud into the juice, brace yourself and apply directly to the ulcer. A slightly milder version uses essential oils. Three drops of tea-tree oil, two of myrrh oil and three of lemon oil are required, with a little almond oil. Apply either with a cotton bud or your clean finger, directly onto the ulcer, at two hourly intervals. This will numb, disinfect and kill bacteria all in one go.

Digestion Aid

Poor digestion can lead to constipation. Lemon juice in hot water, with a little honey added, can be taken each morning to aid the digestive system. Lemons have potassium, minerals and Vitamin C and other natural ingredients, all of which help cleanse the body.

Indigestion

Baking soda is known to be an effective antacid, so it can work for most stomach discomforts, particularly things like indigestion and heartburn, which can make you feel really uncomfortable.

If you are one of those unfortunate people who regularly suffer from that bloated feeling after a meal, try sprinkling a little baking soda on to your food. It helps to reduce the build-up of gas that causes the bloated feeling. You can use baking soda whenever you've got excessive bloating for whatever reason.

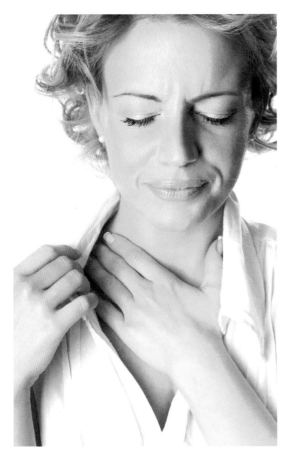

Some foods and drinks can give you heartburn every time you eat or drink them. But you don't have to suffer in silence or give up consuming them. Add 1 teaspoon baking soda to a glass of water and the burning feeling will disappear really quickly.

Other types of food, perhaps those that are greasy or really rich, can give you an upset stomach. This is particularly true if you don't make a habit of eating a good old fry-up. When you do, try adding 1 teaspoon baking soda to your glass of water and the churning in the stomach soon settles down.

The acids in lemon juice help emulsify fats, particularly those in fried food. This can certainly help prevent indigestion, for people who are prone to it or those that have insufficient stomach acid. This is particularly the case for people over the age of 60 years. By ensuring you include lemons in your daily diet, indigestion can certainly be a thing of the past.

The acetic acid in vinegar is said to help prevent the naturally important hydrochloric acid, which is vital in the process of food digestion, from leaving the stomach too quickly. Food is digested more completely with less 'reflux', belching, 'wind' or indigestion pains. Instead of a chemical indigestion remedy, 1 teaspoon apple cider vinegar mixed with 1–2 teaspoons honey in a glass of water may do the job just as well.

Nausea

Just smelling a lemon can often help reduce that feeling of nausea. Whether it is because of something you have eaten, too much alcohol, or even car sickness, make sure you cut open a lemon and take a deep breath. It should soothe your stomach and get rid of that churning feeling.

Constipation and Diarrhea

To help ease constipation, as soon as you get up in the morning, boil the kettle and squeeze the juice of a whole lemon into a mug. Top this juice up with hot water. Make sure you drink it while it is still warm, at least 30 minutes before you eat breakfast. Repeat this at night before going to bed.

Lemons can also help in exactly the opposite way, as they are useful in helping to deal with diarrhea. The pectin in lemons helps to bind the bowel contents and also forms a coating, which soothes irritation. The cellulose in lemons attracts water, which makes the contents of the bowel bulkier.

Lemons are used in West Africa to help protect against cholera, due to the citric acid they contain. The acidity of lemons is very similar to that of stomach acid, so this makes lemons very useful if you do not produce much stomach acid naturally. To help your bowel, make sure you include lemon juice and the zest as part of your daily diet.

Hemorrhoids

Hemorrhoids can be extremely painful and debilitating. The spongy pads can become inflamed, itch and bleed. They can be caused by fragile veins or constipation. The fiber in a lemon helps to prevent constipation and the Vitamin C strengthens the veins. Lemons are also known for their anti-inflammatory antioxidants, which are good for reducing inflammation.

There are two ways of tackling piles with lemon juice. Squeeze the juice of half a lemon into a glass of water and drink it first thing in the morning, before your bathroom visit. At bedtime try mixing ½ tbsp of lemon juice with a similar amount of glycerine, then dab the mixture onto the hemorrhoids each night to help soothe.

Urine Infection

Urinary infections, or cystitis, are painful and can make you feel really miserable. To get rid of it you need to reduce acidifying foods and increase alkalizing foods. Lemons can help with this process. Squeeze the juice of a lemon into a glass of warm water and drink this first thing in the morning. It will change the pH of the urinary tract and discourage the proliferation of bad bacteria, which cause the inflammation of the mucous membranes and walls of the urinary tract.

You should make sure that you also drink a lot of filtered water each day. Add cranberries and blueberries to your diet and certainly avoid alcohol, fizzy soft drinks, tomatoes, yeast, sugar and artificial sweeteners. With the exception of the lemon juice you should also avoid other citrus fruits while the infection remains. Believe it or not, the citric acid in the lemon juice will have an alkalizing effect on the urinary tract. It will also reduce inflammation while cleansing and cooling, as well as operating as an astringent and antiseptic.

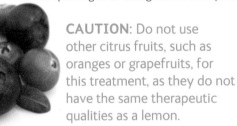

CAUTION: Do not use other citrus fruits, such as oranges or grapefruits, for this treatment, as they do not have the same therapeutic qualities as a lemon.

Urine Retention

Squeezing half a lemon into a glass of water is a simple remedy for eliminating fluid retention. Strange though it may seem, in order to prevent water retention you need to drink more water. It is usually the case that the body retains water when we are dehydrated. By drinking up to 10 glasses of water a day most cases of water retention will be eliminated. You should avoid food that has additional sodium, such as salt.

CAUTION: You should not eliminate all sodium from your diet. Switch to fresher food, particularly vegetables, rather than adding salt to the diet.

Cramps

Lemon tea is often taken as a cure for stomach cramps. Some recommend squeezing the juice of a lemon and then infusing a curry leaf, with a pinch of sugar. This can be consumed as an instant relief for stomach pains of all kinds.

Fibroids

Women with an imbalance of estrogen and progesterone may often be prone to the growth of womb muscle fibers, known as fibroids. This is also true if an individual is overweight, because fat cells also produce estrogen.

The fiber in a lemon helps to encourage the re-absorption of estrogen from the bowel and into the blood and the B vitamins present help the liver to break down the estrogen. So including the juice and zest of a lemon in a daily diet can have an impact on fibroids.

Stimulating or Suppressing Appetite

Surprisingly, a lemon can help to both stimulate and suppress appetite. Lemon juice and water taken first thing in the morning will reduce and suppress your appetite initially because it fills up the stomach – it also picks you up and makes you feel more alert – but it can also stimulate the appetite, as it stimulates digestion and liver function, as well as detoxifying and cleansing the bowel.

Detox Diets

There are various recipes for a lemon juice detox. Keep any of the following mixtures stored in the refrigerator.

The most well-known recipe is to prepare a cup of hot water and squeeze in the juice of a whole lemon. Add sugar or honey to taste. The lemon juice needs to be taken first thing in the morning and throughout the day you should be sure to consume plenty of water. It is thought that the lemon juice flushes out toxins, particularly from the liver.

In another recipe, a cup of cold, filtered water is used, along with 2 tbsp of fresh lemon juice, 2 tbsp of organic maple syrup and a pinch or two of cayenne pepper. This lemon detox diet recommends that 6 to 12 of these servings are consumed every day.

A slightly less extreme version is designed to last for just two days. Mix together 500 ml/18 fl oz/ 2 cups of lemon juice, 1 litre/1¾ pints/4 cups of orange juice and 1.5 litres/2½ pints/6⅓ cups of grapefruit juice. Water down the mixture to the strength you prefer. Drink one cup every hour until the whole of your two-day mixture has been consumed.

The downside of these detox diets is that you cannot have anything to eat during their duration. It is not recommended that you continue any of these diets for more than seven days.

CAUTION: A lemon detox diet is quite extreme and if taken alone will lead to weight loss.

Metabolic Rate Increase

The lemon detox diet is specifically designed to encourage an increase in the metabolic rate (which measures how quickly your body converts food into energy), to burn up body fat, while cleansing, detoxifying and rejuvenating the body.

During a lemon detox diet the natural process of ridding the body of toxins continues, but you are not taking any more toxins into your body. At the same time, any energy that you would normally use to digest your food is re-routed to promote cell growth and improve your immune system. As a result the immune system does not need to work as hard as usual and your digestive system is not susceptible to inflammation due to allergic reactions to food. At the same time any chemicals in your system, such as pesticides or drugs, are flushed out.

Stomach, Liver and Intestines

These are all linked to your metabolic rate (which measures how quickly your body converts food into energy). The thyroid gland determines your metabolic rate. The lemon juice and water mix taken first thing in the morning will certainly get the digestive system working, as well as encouraging liver function. Bitter foods in any case stimulate liver and gall-bladder function. The lemon will also help give your intestines a super clean. Again this is a variation on the lemon detox diet, which incorporates lemon juice, organic maple syrup, a pinch of cayenne pepper and filtered water (see pages 202–203). This will help flush through your intestines while providing you with a range of vitamins and minerals. You could do the lemon detox diet drink on a daily basis to cleanse the colon.

Gall Stones

Gall stones are formed in the gall bladder by stagnant bile, or calcium salts. They are often associated with diabetes, constipation and obesity and are much more common if you have an unhealthy diet.

The pectin in a lemon should stop bile acids from the gut being re-absorbed, which helps to prevent gall stones from forming. The lemon juice alone should also encourage the gall bladder to contract and flush out bile and small gall stones.

You can give your gall bladder a thorough flushing by following a fairly extreme, but effective, regime. For six days drink 1 litre/1¾ pints/4 cups of apple juice and on the seventh day take 2 tbsp of Epsom salts in water. Wait one hour and then take 120 ml/4 fl oz/½ cup of olive oil with 4

tbsp of lemon juice. You should then lie on the left side of your body for 30 minutes before going to bed for the night. The theory is that the flush will not only encourage the gall bladder to contract, but it will also soften any gall stones that may be present.

As a less extreme treatment, take 1 tbsp of lemon juice mixed with an equal amount of olive oil an hour before eating each morning. This is thought to help the body break down gall stones, as well as encouraging the contraction of the gall bladder. A contracted gall bladder helps expel any gall stones that are present.

If you are prone to gall stones you should certainly consider incorporating at least two lemons in your daily diet.

CAUTION: Always consult your doctor if any painful symptoms persist.

Kidney Stones

Lemon juice is a diuretic, which encourages the production of urine. Lemons also have citric acid, which encourages the liver to create enzymes.

Lemons can help prevent kidney stones from forming, as they provide Vitamin B, fiber, magnesium, calcium and selenium. Lemon juice can also help dissolve existing stones. Some stones are made up of calcium and they are formed because the body fluids are too acidic. The lemon juice has an alkaline effect on the body.

People with raised blood-sugar levels produce additional insulin, particularly after they eat carbohydrates. This makes the kidneys flush out calcium into the urine. The acidity in a lemon helps to prevent this, so as a preventative measure, incorporate lemons into your daily diet.

To help reduce the excruciating pain that can result from the presence of a kidney stone, squeeze the juice of half a lemon into a glass of water. Drink this mixture and repeat every 30 minutes until the pain is reduced.

Heart Palpitations

Heart palpitations are common and often caused by a poor diet, or stress. Physical activity, smoking and anxiety can also be key triggers for heart palpitations, which can give you an increased pulse rate and a thumping feeling in the chest.

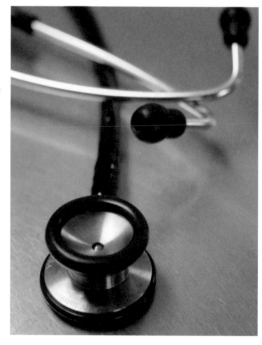

Lemons can again come to the rescue. There are two similar treatments you could try. Squeeze out half a cup of lemon juice and add 1 tbsp of honey. Dilute this mixture with water. Ideally take this mixture before going to bed, but it is also a good general remedy to help you get a feeling of calm.

An alternative is to take the juice of half a lemon and half a lime, along with the honey. Then add 250 ml/8 fl oz/1 cup of water. Take this mixture on a daily basis in order to reduce the likelihood of feeling stressed.

CAUTION: Do not ignore heart palpitations. If they persist contact your doctor.

Baby Care

Because baking soda is not harmful to children and babies, it is the perfect way to keep the nursery clean and fresh-smelling. Baking soda, and vinegar too, can be used for many baby-related tasks. It can be used to clean baby and his or her toys, as well as to eliminate those sometimes overpowering baby smells around the home. You can use baking soda with confidence around baby; it contains nothing that can irritate the skin or cause any allergic reactions.

Cleansing & Treatments

Baby Bath

Adding 200 g/7 oz/1 cup of baking soda to baby's bath can help keep their skin wonderfully soft. You can use it instead of a bubble bath and rest easy that it won't irritate baby's skin.

Cleaning Bath Toys

Baby's bath toys can get a build-up of limescale. To remove this, sprinkle some baking soda on to a damp cloth and scrub clean. The baking soda also eliminates any lingering smells on the toys.

For really stubborn limescale on the toys you could make a paste of baking soda and water and scrub with an old toothbrush.

Diaper Rash Treatment

Diaper rash can be so uncomfortable for baby. If you've tried all the proprietary brands and they've not worked, try putting 1–2 teaspoons baking soda in the bath water after you've washed baby's face. The baking soda soothes baby's bottom and helps prevent diaper rash coming back.

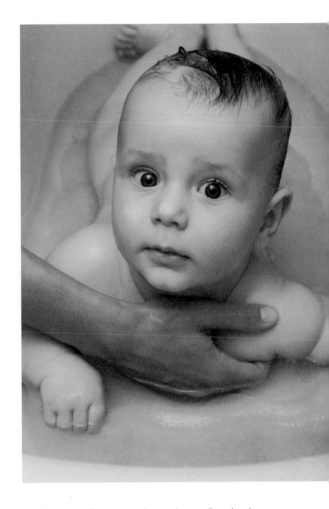

If the diaper rash is causing serious discomfort you can use baking soda at every diaper change. Dissolve 1 teaspoon in a cup of warm water and apply it to baby's bottom. Apply the mixture around the whole of the affected area and allow the mixture to air-dry naturally.

Irritation is also very often caused by the soap residues in cloth diapers and underwear: rinse these in a mild solution of water and white vinegar – about 120 ml/4 fl oz/½ cup to 2.3 litres/4 pints/9⅔ cups of water to neutralize the alkaline of the soap and balance the pH level.

Cradle Cap Treatment

To effectively remove what can be unsightly cradle cap, mix together some baking soda and water. Smear it on to the affected area about an hour before bath time then rinse the mixture off in the bath.

Adding some baking soda to olive oil is another cradle cap treatment. Mix the two together and apply to the affected area by smearing it on. It is quite messy so use old sheets if you can. But it is effective at removing the cradle cap.

Thrush in the Mouth Treatment

If baby is suffering from thrush in the mouth, which is quite common in infants, mix together ¼ teaspoon baking soda, 250 ml/8 fl oz/1 cup water and a drop of liquid soap. Using a spotlessly clean cotton cloth dab the mixture on to baby's tongue 4–6 times a day. It won't hurt baby.

Cleaning & Odor Removal

Crib and Playpen

Because baking soda is not harmful to children or babies, it can be used to freshen up their room. It deodorizes smells and leaves the whole room smelling fresh. Baby's crib can often get quite grimy, particularly when they start pulling themselves up. To get rid of finger marks and grease, use a mixture of 100 g/4 oz/½ cup baking soda, 50 ml/2 fl oz/¼ cup white vinegar and 2.25 litres/4 pints/2¼ qts warm water. This mixture will get rid of smells in the crib too.

Any urine smells lingering in the nursery or child's room can be eliminated by sprinkling some baking soda on to the mattress of the crib or the bed when changing the sheets.

The playpen can get just as mucky, if not more so, than the crib. And the playpen often has lingering food, vomit and urine smells. Use the same mixture as for cleaning the crib. This will deodorize the playpen and make it a nicer place for baby to play.

Toy Box

You can clean baby's toy box too. Once a month mix together 200 g/7 oz/1 cup baking soda with an equal quantity of white vinegar. Use the mixture to clean the toy box and wipe all toys made of suitable material.

Soft Toys

Baking soda works on soft toys and stuffed animals just as well. Put them in a clean pillowcase and add some baking soda, which you should sprinkle over the toys. If you give them a good shake they'll come out smelling as fresh as daisies.

Crayon Marks

It is going to happen as your baby starts to get mobile – crayon on the walls and paintwork. Mix up a paste of baking soda and water. With an old toothbrush apply the paste to the mark – magic, it's gone!

Bottles

Put a couple of tablespoons of baking soda in baby's bottles and fill them with water. Leave them overnight to soak and the sour smells will disappear.

If your baby's bottles can be put in the dishwasher, add some baking soda to the powder or tablet area. This will ensure that the dishwasher is clean enough to wash baby's bottles.

Teats and Pacifiers

When teats and pacifiers are not in use they can be kept in cold water to which a pinch of baking soda has been added.

Teats and pacifiers can get discolored and stained, particularly when baby has moved on to solids. To remove the stains mix a weak paste of baking soda and water, and give them a good scrub. Rinse well afterwards.

Washing Cloth Diapers

Some babies can get an allergy to washing powder that can cause diaper rash. Try putting 200 g/7 oz/1 cup of baking soda in the wash to help avoid this.

The washing powder you use regularly can build up on diapers and baby clothes over time. To eliminate the build-up of the washing powder, replace it for one wash with 200 g/7 oz/1 cup baking soda. Use similar quantities to your washing powder. It won't lather so much but it will reduce the build-up.

You can keep your diapers looking bright and white if you add 100 g/4 oz/½ cup baking soda to your washing machine. Put it in the powder chamber of your machine and you'll be proud to hang those white diapers out to dry!

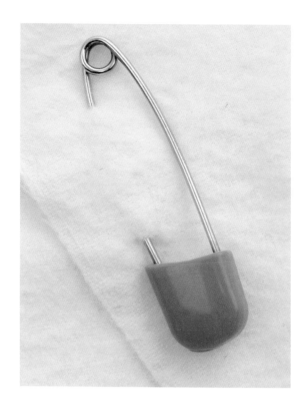

Diaper Bucket

If you use terry or cloth diapers, the bucket will inevitably get smelly. Sprinkle some baking soda (about 200 g/7 oz/1 cup) over each diaper as you add it to the bucket. This will deodorize the smells until washday.

Deodorizing Clothes

To eliminate baby smells from their clothes, and from your own, add 100 g/4 oz/½ cup baking soda to water and soak the clothes for a few hours before washing.

If baby's clothes don't need a wash, but just need to be freshened up, you can sprinkle them with some baking soda to deodorize any lingering odors. Leave them overnight if you can and the stale smells will be gone by the morning.

Food

Culinary Basics

The lemon probably ranks third after salt and pepper as the most common and useful culinary ingredient. You can use lemon to bring out the taste of meat and vegetables, to brighten up a dish, to unleash flavors and to make sauces, seasonings and attractive accompaniments. Lemons can be squeezed, peeled, zested or dried. They can even be cooked. In addition to using baking soda in recipes, baking soda can also be used in a number of ways to prepare foodstuffs or to preserve them. And let's not forget vinegar's invaluable use in food preparation and flavoring.

Lemon Seasonings

Lemon Zest and Lemon Pepper

You can easily make your own lemon zest, or even pep it up by making a lemon and pepper mix, which is brilliant for seasoning chicken and a host of other foods, as well as being perfect for the grill.

1   Using a zester or a vegetable peeler, remove the yellow zest, taking care not to remove any of the white pith, which can taste sour.

2   When you have removed the zest mince it up and put it into a small bowl.

3   Optionally you can then add two teaspoons of peppercorns. You will need to crack them first with a mortar and pestle, or by putting them onto a cutting board and bashing them with a heavy-based pot or a rolling pin.

4   Mix the zest and cracked pepper together and this will encourage the lemon oils to combine with the pepper.

5   Now spread the zest and pepper onto a baking sheet and leave it in a very low-heat oven overnight to dry out. Or dry it by spreading it on a towel and leaving it until dried.

6   Put the dry mix into a mortar and pestle and pulverize it. Now it is ready to be sprinkled onto your dish, perhaps fish or chicken. To boost the flavor you can squeeze fresh lemon juice over the dish just before cooking. The zest will store well in an airtight jar and you can also freeze it.

CAUTION: Unless you are absolutely certain about the source of your lemons, scrub the fruit with a sponge and warm, soapy water before you zest it. This will release any wax or dirt. Rinse well and dry with a paper towel.

Lemon Extract

If you have plenty of time on your hands you can make your own lemon extract. Put the peel of three or four lemons into about 120 ml/4 fl oz/½ cup of water. Place it in a pan and allow it to simmer for a while. Strain the peel, but continue to reduce the liquid to concentrate the flavor. You should get around 2 tbsp of lemony liquid.

Lemon Extract Powder

You can also make lemon extract powder by removing the peel from lemons, making sure that you do not cut off any of the pith. Dry the strips skin-side down on a plate until they are thoroughly dry. This should take about three or four days. Once dry you can pulverize them in a blender, or use a pestle and mortar. Use the powdered peel in a host of different recipes.

Lemon Sugar

There are two simple ways of making your own lemon sugar. You can use lemon extract powder (see above) and simply add it to the sugar, or you can use lemon twists. Lemon twists are like zested lemon peel, except you use a vegetable peeler to make long strips. Pop some of these twists into a jar with your sugar, and the lemon oil from the peel will infuse into the sugar. Replace the twists when you refill your sugar canister.

Candied Lemon Peel

The tangy flavor of candied lemon peel is so straightforward to make and is a wonderful alternative to confectionery. It is also a brilliant homemade gift, as well as having the added bonus of being fat-free!

1   Use a knife or citrus peeler to produce long strips of lemon peel. You will probably need to use at least six lemons. Make sure that you try to avoid any of the bitter, white pith.

2   Combine 900 ml/1½ pints/ scant 4 cups of water with 2½ cups of sugar. Cook on a medium heat on top of the stove, stirring until the sugar is dissolved. Then allow the mixture to boil for five minutes.

3   Drop in the strips of peel and reduce the heat to a simmer. Continue to cook, but do not stir, until the syrup is reduced to around a quarter. This could take up to two hours.

4   Remove your pan from the heat and allow the liquid to cool before draining the lemon peel. Preheat your oven up to 200°C/400°F/Gas Mark 6.

5   Carefully retrieve each of the peels, one by one, and dunk them into a bowl of sugar. You need to ensure that each one is fully coated.

6   Place the peels on a baking sheet lined with baking parchment. Allow the sugar-coated peels to dry out in the hot oven, which will take around an hour. Make sure you check to ensure that they are not burning.

7   When the peels are completely dry you can scrape off any excess sugar. They should now keep for around a week. As a special treat, why not try dipping the candied peel into melted chocolate!

Preserved Lemons

Salting lemons can take away much of their sourness and you can then store them in oil.

You will need:
around 15 small lemons (unwaxed)
3 tbsp salt
2 tbsp paprika
4 bay leaves
720 ml/24 fl oz/3 cups hazelnut or walnut oil

1   Wash and slice the lemons, then layer them in a colander and sprinkle salt on each layer. Leave the lemons for 24 hours and dry them with a paper towel.

2   Prepare a preserving jar by sterilizing it first by putting it in a hot oven for at least 10 minutes.

3   Begin filling the jar with the slices of lemon. Each layer should have a sprinkle of paprika. Every three or four layers add a bay leaf.

4   When you have finished layering the lemons cover with the oil and seal the jar. Store it in a cool, dark place.

You can use the lemons immediately, but once the jar is opened it should be stored in a refrigerator. The lemons should be fine for the next six months.

Alternatively you could store the unopened jar for around two years. These preserved lemons are wonderful in stews and they make great holiday gifts.

Meat & Poultry Tips

Free of Feathers

Sometimes when you buy a chicken there are a few feathers left on the skin. They won't do you any harm, but they can be a bit off-putting. To get rid of these quickly and easily just rub the skin of the chicken with baking soda. Rinse the baking soda off before cooking the bird.

Kill Germs

Lightly wiping raw meat with a little vinegar or lemon juice will help to eradicate bacteria. The acid will change the pH of the meat, which could make it a more hostile environment for bacteria and thus help to preserve it.

Tone Down Flavor

You can use baking soda to reduce the strong flavor of meats such as venison, particularly if you are planning to preserve the meat. Add the baking soda to your preserving jar to get rid of an overwhelming flavor.

No Fowl Smell

If you are plucking and preparing your own chicken you can get rid of the sometimes strong smell by sprinkling some baking soda into the cavity before drawing out the giblets.

Tenderize and Marinate Meat

Baking soda is also really good for tenderizing chicken meat. Rub the meat liberally with some baking soda and then rinse it thoroughly for a really tender chicken.

You can add ½ teaspoon baking soda to your meat marinade prior to cooking stir-fry dishes. The baking soda will help soften the texture of the meat, particularly if the meat you've bought is one of the tougher cuts. The meat will melt in your mouth.

If you have tough, chewy meat then you can marinade it in lemon juice overnight. The juice will break down muscle tissue, making the meat much more tender. The flavor-enhancing lemon will also add to any meat dish, especially those using chicken or lamb. Try using a marinade of lemon juice, olive oil and oregano next time you grill some meat.

Add 1 tablespoon of a vinegar, such as red wine or cider vinegar, to stews and casseroles to help tenderize the meat. When marinating meat, add 1 tablespoon vinegar to the marinade which again will help to tenderize.

Crispy Chicken

If you want the chicken skin to be crispy you can rub in some baking soda or rub a lemon over the skin before cooking. Crispy skin and tender meat – delicious!

Pork Crackling

If you like your pork crackling really crisp, then baking soda can do this for you. Sprinkle and smear some baking soda on to the pork skin before cooking. The baking soda will help the skin to really crisp up for you. Score the skin as usual, with crisscross cuts using a sharp knife. Cutting like this helps to crisp up the skin too and makes it easier to cut and share, because everyone will want some!

Smearing baking soda on to the skin of your pork meat will not only give you a crispy crackling, but it will also help keep the meat tender too.

Vegetable Tips

Vibrant Carrots

Even if carrots are past their best they can be rejuvenated by adding a little baking soda to the cooking water. Adding the baking soda has a double effect; it helps the color and helps keep them crisp too.

White Cauliflower

Two tablespoons baking soda added to the cooking water when you are boiling a cauliflower will help keep the flower of the vegetable nice and white.

Great Greens

To maintain the color of green vegetables you can add ½ teaspoon baking soda to the cooking water. This works really well for green beans, broccoli and sprouts. Don't forget that you should never overcook your greens – if you do, most of the goodness ends up in the water.

Prevent Vegetables (and Fruit!) from Turning Brown

As soon as we cut vegetables such as potatoes, sweet potatoes, parsnips, and artichokes, or fruits such as apples, pears and bananas, they start to turn brown. This is because enzymes in their cells are exposed to and react with the oxygen in the air. Simply squeeze a little lemon juice over vegetables or freshly cut fruit while you are preparing them and they will retain their original, vibrant color.

If you are into making smoothies you may have noticed exactly the same browning problem. It look less appetizing, even though it may still taste delicious. Just add a few drops of lemon juice into the smoothie-maker or electric juicer for all the original colors to be retained.

Keep Lettuce Crisp

Lemon juice can be used to stop a lettuce from going limp or from browning after you've cut it. To revive your lettuce drop it into a bowl of cold water that has had the juice of half a lemon added. Pop the bowl into your refrigerator for an hour and the lettuce will recover and be fresh and crispy again.

Crisp Corn

If you want to keep your corn on the cob crisp, why not try adding 2 tablespoons baking soda to the cooking water?

First Class Cabbage

To reduce the cooking time of cabbage and to keep it tender, you just have to add 3 tablespoons baking soda to the cooking water. We all agree that there's nothing worse than overcooked cabbage!

Adding baking soda to your cabbage's cooking water can also help your family and friends avoid the ill effects of the vegetable's gasses after eating the meal. Must be much better for all concerned, we're sure you'll agree!

CAUTION: Although baking soda has a positive visual effect on vegetables, don't be tempted to add too much or get into a habit of using it all the time, as it arguably can destroy the natural vitamins C and B1 in the veggies.

Enhance the Flavor of Mushrooms

The natural, earthy taste of mushrooms is enhanced by squeezing a little lemon juice over them as they cook. This works regardless of the method of cooking you are using.

Soaking Beans

If you like to eat dried beans but want to soften them before cooking, you can help them along when soaking them overnight by adding 1 teaspoon baking soda to the water – with enough water to cover the beans fully.

No More Beans Blues

You know how the saying goes: 'beans, beans are good for your heart, the more you eat ...' Well, to solve the excess gas problem try adding 1 teaspoon baking soda to your baked beans when you are cooking them. All of the bean goodness is there without the unpleasant aftereffects!

Clean Veg

You can't be too careful when it comes to food handling and preparation. Wash your fruit and vegetables in cold water with 2–3 tablespoons baking soda added to it. This will help remove some of the impurities that our tap water leaves behind.

For more thorough cleaning, the dirt in or on your fruit and vegetables will wash away so much quicker and easier if you add 100 g/4 oz/½ cup baking soda to the water.

To go further, if you want to be sure your shop-bought vegetables are chemical-free when you cook them, try washing them with 200 g/7 oz/1 cup baking soda added to a sinkful of fresh water. More and more of the ready-prepared vegetables and fruits look too good to be true – shiny fruit is often covered with edible wax, but baking soda will get rid of this for you.

Alternatively, you can dab a wet sponge or your vegetables brush into neat baking soda and use this to scrub your vegetables. The baking soda will remove the dirt, any wax and pesticides. Give everything a thorough rinsing before serving or cooking your vegetables.

Milder Veg

In order to remove the harsher and stronger flavor from some wild vegetables, add around 1 teaspoon baking soda per 1 litre/1¾ pints/1 qt water when you boil your vegetables. The color of the vegetables also becomes brighter.

Speedy Tomatoes

If you are making your own tomato sauce or salsa, you can reduce the cooking time by adding some baking soda. Add 2 tablespoons baking soda for every 900 ml/1½ pints/1 qt cooking water. This can reduce the cooking time by at least 10 minutes.

Sweeter Tomatoes

Adding baking soda to the water you are cooking your tomatoes in when preparing your salsa or tomato sauce can also help to neutralize the acid in the tomatoes.

Other Culinary Tips

Soften Brown Sugar

Add lemon peel, making sure that you have removed the pith and all of the pulp, to brown sugar. It will keep the sugar moist and easier to use or blend.

Keep Guacamole Green

Have you ever noticed that when you cut or mash an avocado to make guacamole it begins to turn brown very quickly? The same can be said about cut apples, bananas or pears. Sprinkling some fresh lemon juice over the fruit will keep it fresh and green for much longer and the lemon juice will only add to the taste of your guacamole.

Make Sour Milk

To make sour milk or sour cream simply squeeze a little lemon juice into fresh milk or cream.

Whip Cream

You know how sometimes whipping cream just will not whip? Try adding a few drops of lemon juice to solve the problem.

Prevent Sticky Rice

Interestingly, lemon juice, when added to the water when you are cooking rice, makes the rice fluffy and also helps prevent grains from sticking together and clogging.

Stop Boiled Eggs from Cracking

If you dab egg shells with lemon juice or vinegar before you pop them into boiling water then the shells should not crack. To be doubly sure you could also add some more lemon juice or vinegar (about 2 teaspoons) to the boiling water. This will also make it easier to peel the eggs.

Make Perfect Poached Eggs

To make sure that your poached eggs are perfect, squeeze a few drops of lemon juice or distilled white or white wine vinegar into the boiling water. Swirl the water around and then drop in the eggs. This will help to keep the white intact.

General Flavor Enhancer

Add a zing to boring bland dishes by adding 2–3 teaspoons vinegar. Try balsamic and look for the different balsamic flavors.

Keep Food Longer

Vinegar acts as a preserver – olives when covered in white wine vinegar and kept covered in the refrigerator will keep indefinitely.

De-glazing the Pan

Add 1–2 tablespoons vinegar to de-glaze a frying or roasting pan. (Adding liquid to the dried and caramelized meat juices in the pan after cooking meat provides a delicious jus or gravy when combined with the meat juices.)

Cut Through Grease

When eating fried food, such as potato wedges and fries, sprinkle with a few drops of vinegar to remove the greasy taste and feel to the mouth. Some will argue that it helps your body 'break down the fat' too!

Clean Pudding Pans

When steaming a pudding add a few drops of vinegar to the water in the bottom of the pan. This will keep the pan clean.

A Question of Taste

If you live in a hard-water area, perhaps you don't like the taste of your tap water? To improve the taste you could add 1 teaspoon baking soda to each 2.25 litres/4 pints/2¼ qts tap water.

Neutralize Acidity

If you suffer with stomach ulcers, it is important that you don't consume too much acid. There is plenty of citric acid in most fruits that can upset and inflame the stomach. You can neutralize the acid in coffee by adding 1 teaspoon baking soda to your cup or mug. Why not add it to the coffee pot when you make a fresh brew? Two or 3 teaspoons baking soda will be more than enough for everyone.

Good Practice

Resist the urge to add more baking soda or baking powder than a recipe instructs, as this can cause the food to taste bitter and it can also cause the bread or cake to rise too rapidly so that the air bubbles grow too large and burst, which in turn causes the mixture to collapse. On the other hand, too little baking powder or baking soda leads to a tough and densely textured product.

Baking Powder

Ever noticed how some recipes call for baking soda while others call for baking powder? As discussed in the Introduction, these are two different things. However, you can make your own baking powder by stirring and sifting together two parts cream of tartar to one part baking soda and one part cornstarch.

Basic Recipes

Lemonade

There are two ways of making lemonade. One is slightly sweeter than the other.

You will need:

3 lemons, pips removed, sliced
100 g/3½ oz/½ cup superfine sugar
2 x 570 ml/20 fl oz/2¼ cups boiled water

1   Put the lemon, sugar and the first batch of boiled water into a blender and blitz until smooth.

2   Then stir in the second batch of boiled water. Strain into a pitcher. You can drink it warm or pop it in the refrigerator and add ice cubes just before serving.

If you do not have a blender then put the lemon slices and sugar directly into the pitcher. Add all the boiled water at the same time, which should have just finished boiling. Stir the mixture with a wooden spoon until all the sugar is dissolved, squashing the lemon slices on the side of the pitcher to make sure you have released all the flavor. Strain the lemonade into a second pitcher.

If you prefer a less bitter lemon taste, follow the same steps, but this time zest the three lemons and squeeze the juice out of them, rather than slicing them, and discard the pith.

Lemon Barley Water

This is similar to the lemonade recipes on the previous page.

You will need:
1.7 litres/3 pints/7 cups boiled water
75g /3 oz/⅓ cup pearl or wild barley
3 lemons, chopped
50 g/2 oz/¼ cup sugar

1   Put the water and barley into a pan and bring it to a boil. Cover the pan and allow the mixture to simmer for half an hour.

2   Drop in the lemons and sugar and stir to dissolve the sugar before allowing the whole mixture to cool down.

3   Once it has cooled sufficiently strain it into a pitcher. Store your lemon barley water in the refrigerator, where it should last for up to five days.

As an alternative, you can use 150 g/5 oz/¾ cup of pearl barley, the grated zest and juice of two lemons, 165 g/5½ oz/½ cup of honey and 1.5 litres/2½ pints/6⅓ cups of water. First rinse the barley in a strainer and then pour the water, lemon zest and barley into a pan. Bring the mixture to a boil and allow it to simmer for 10 minutes before straining it into a bowl. Now add the honey and stir until it is fully dissolved before stirring in the lemon juice. For an additional kick, finely grate a tablespoonful of fresh ginger and add it at the beginning of the process.

Lemon Sorbet

Lemon sorbet is exceptionally good for cleansing the palate. It is also a really easy dessert, as long as you have enough time to wait for it to set in the freezer. You can make your own lemon sorbet, with or without limoncello (an Italian lemon vodka). You can also add your own, special ingredients – even champagne for an extra special occasion!

You will need:
570 ml/20 fl oz/2¼ cups water
25 g/80 oz/2 tbsp superfine sugar
5 or 6 lemons (juice only, plus the peel from just
   3 of them)
2 tbsp limoncello (optional)
2 egg whites

1   Pour the water into a pan and add the sugar. Cook on a medium heat until the sugar is dissolved.

2   Drop in the peel from 3 of your lemons and allow the mixture to simmer for 10 minutes before removing the peel.

3   Pour in the lemon juice and the limoncello, (if using) then pour the whole mixture into a freezable container.

4   Once it is cool, freeze it for 2 hours. The mixture should now be mushy and not frozen solid. Take a fork, stir up the partially frozen mixture.

5   Whisk the egg whites, making sure they form firm peaks.

6   Fold the egg whites into the sorbet thoroughly and put the container back into the freezer for around 4 hours. Take the container out of the freezer for around 30 minutes before serving.

For that added wow factor, why not serve your lemon sorbet in lemons? Just cut off the top third of the lemon, which will become the lid. Hollow out the lemon and the lid and cut a small slice out of the bottom of each lemon so it can stand upright. Put the lemons and the lids in the freezer and after a couple of hours they should harden up. When you are ready to serve the sorbet take them out, fill them with the sorbet, replace the lid and hey presto, no dishwashing!

Lemon Curd

Lemon curd is a useful addition to a number of recipes.

You will need:
125 g/4 oz/½ cup (1 stick) unsalted butter
juice and zest of 3 lemons
220 g/7 oz/heaping 1 cup superfine sugar
6 egg yolks

1   Melt the butter in a saucepan and whisk in the lemon juice, zest and sugar.

2   Add the egg yolks and whisk until the mixture is smooth. Continue to heat and stir for up to 15 minutes. You are looking for a consistency that will coat your wooden spoon, but do not allow it to boil.

3   Remove the mixture from the heat and pour into a sterilized preserving jar. Allow the mixture to cool in the jar to room temperature and then store it in the refrigerator. You can also put the lemon curd into a plastic container and store it in the freezer for two months.

Lemon Salad Dressing

One of the simplest salad dressings takes full advantage of the sensation of tangy, fresh lemon.

You will need:
2 tbsp lemon juice
1 tsp mustard powder
a little honey
6 tbsp olive oil
salt and pepper

Combine all of the ingredients in a jar and give it a vigorous shake. You can also add freshly chopped herbs of your choice: basil, parsley, thyme or oregano work perfectly. Your salad dressing is now ready to annoint your salad.

Hot Lemon Punch

This is a great winter warmer that combines red wine, tea, orange, lemon, honey, sugar and spices.

You will need:
1.1 litres/2 pints/4⅔ cups boiled water
2 tea bags
juice and zest of 1 lemon and 1 orange
1 cinnamon stick
3 cloves
570 ml/20 fl oz/2¼ cups of red wine
1 tbsp sugar (you may wish to add more to taste
   if you have a sweet tooth)
2 tbsp honey

1   Take a large pan and pour in the water and drop in the tea bags. Allow the tea bags to infuse for around 30 minutes.

2   Take out the tea bags and drop in the lemon and orange zest and juice, along with the cloves and cinnamon stick. Stir well and allow this to infuse for around 30 minutes before adding the wine, sugar and honey.

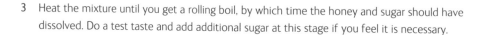

3   Heat the mixture until you get a rolling boil, by which time the honey and sugar should have dissolved. Do a test taste and add additional sugar at this stage if you feel it is necessary.

Make Vinegar from Scratch

The Mother
First you need the 'vinegar mother': place 2 tablespoons vinegar and half a bottle of wine or cider in a bowl and leave for 2 weeks uncovered in a sunny position. The skin that forms is the 'acetobacter' or 'mother'. This is your starter.

Take Time

Skim off the 'mother' and place it with more of the same wine or cider originally used into a clean bowl, ensuring that the 'mother' remains on top. Cover with muslin, or other porous material that will allow plenty of oxygen through while protecting the liquid from insects. Leave in a warm place for 1 month or longer, until you are happy with the taste.

Strain off the vinegar intro a sterile bottle and cork. Add more alcohol to the 'mother' in order to start again – the 'mother' lasts indefinitely, as long as fresh alcohol is 'fed' to it.

Rosemary Vinegar

Makes 600 ml/1 pint/2½ cups
450 g/1 lb fresh rosemary sprigs, rinsed
600 ml/1 pint/2½ cups white wine or cider vinegar

This recipe can be used with a variety of herbs – try tarragon, thyme, bay and oregano. The more delicate herbs such as basil, dill, mint and cilantro will need their leaves bruising slightly. Avoid using dried herbs or spices as

these could make the vinegar cloudy. For maximum flavor, if you grow your own rosemary, pick it first thing in the morning after the dew has dried and before it gets hot. The essential oils are released when it is around 30°C/85°F.

1   Discard the woody stems from the rosemary and place half in a glass bowl. Pour over the vinegar, stir, cover lightly and leave in a cool place for 7 days stirring occasionally.

2   Strain, discarding the rosemary. Repeat with the remaining rosemary and pour the strained vinegar over. Cover lightly and stir occasionally then leave for a further 7 days.

3   Pour through a fine strainer into sterilized bottles. Add 2–3 rinsed sprigs of fresh rosemary and screw down tightly. Store in a dark place.

Rose Vinegar

Makes approx. 600ml/1pint/2½ cups
350 g/12 oz/1½ cups rose petals
approx. 300ml/½ pt/1¼ cups white wine vinegar

This is a delicately flavored vinegar that is perfect to use as a dressing on salads or vegetables. Make sure that you use rose petals that have a perfume. Petals from other edible flowers can be used in this way too: try chrysanthemums, nasturtiums, marigolds or sweet peas.

1   Lightly rinse and dry the petals ensuring that there are no insects or bugs.

2   Place in a sterilized 300 ml/½ pint/1¼ cup-glass jar with a screw lid. Do not pack down too firmly. Cover with white wine vinegar, seal and leave in a sunny place for at least 1 month before using.

Spiced Vinegar

Makes 700 ml/1¼ pints/3 cups
6 tsp peppercorns
3 tsp mustard seeds
2 tsp allspice
1 blade mace
1 large cinnamon stick, bruised
4 fresh bay leaves
1 small piece fresh ginger, chopped
1 tbsp salt
700 ml/1¼ pints/3 cups malt vinegar

This is perfect if wishing to make your own pickles and chutneys. Again you can vary the spices used according to personal preference. White distilled vinegar is often used as it gives a sharper tang, however white wine, red or malt vinegar is fine to use too.

Tie all the spices into a piece of muslin and place in a non-reactive saucepan. Add 230 ml/8 fl oz/1 cup of the vinegar and bring to a boil. Boil for 3 minutes then add the remaining vinegar and boil for a further 3 minutes. Remove from the heat and leave covered for at least 24 hours. Strain into sterilized bottles and screw down.

Classic Vinaigrette

Makes 145 ml/5 fl oz/⅔ cup

4 tbsp olive oil
1½ tbsp white wine vinegar
1–2 tsp sugar, or to taste
freshly ground black pepper to taste
freshly milled rock salt to taste
1 tsp mustard powder
1 tsp superfine sugar, or to taste

This dressing is used universally and can vary immensely according to local tastes and ingredients.

1   Place all the ingredients into a screw top jar and shake until thoroughly blended.

2   Adjust seasoning and sweetness to taste. Use as required.

Store in a cool cupboard, not in the refrigerator, as this will make the olive oil go cloudy. If liked, replace the sugar with 1 teaspoon clear honey; replace 1 tablespoon of the vinegar with either balsamic vinegar, red wine vinegar or a herb vinegar; or add 1–2 teaspoons crushed garlic or finely chopped chili. You can also add 1 tablespoon finely chopped fresh herb.

Hollandaise Sauce

Makes 145 ml/5 fl oz/⅔ cup

2 tbsp tarragon or white wine vinegar
1 tbsp water
2 fresh medium egg yolks
75–100g/1 stick unsalted butter, cut into small dice
freshly milled rock salt and freshly ground black pepper

This is a true classic and is perfect for serving with fish, eggs and vegetables.

1   Boil the vinegar and water together until reduced by about half. Cool.

2   Place the egg yolks in a small bowl and stir in the cooled vinegar solution.

3   Place the bowl over a pan of gently simmering water and heat, whisking until the mixture thickens.

4   Gradually whisk in the butter, whisking well after each addition. Continue until all the butter has been added. Season to taste and if the sauce is too sharp add a little more butter, or if too thick, add a little hot water.

Crème Fraîche Dressing

Makes about 145 ml/ 5 fl oz/⅔ cup

85 ml/3 fl oz/⅓ cup crème fraîche
2 tsp Dijon mustard or to taste
freshly ground black pepper
4 tbsp extra virgin olive oil
2 tbsp champagne or white
   wine vinegar

This makes a delicious change from mayonnaise.

1   Place the crème fraîche, mustard, pepper, olive oil and vinegar in a screw top jar and shake until blended. Use as required.

If liked, fromage frais can be used in place of the crème fraîche.

BBQ Sauce

Makes about 145 ml/5 fl oz/⅔ cup

50 g/2 oz/½ stick butter
1 large onion, peeled and finely chopped
1 tsp tomato purée
2 tbsp herb vinegar such as tarragon or rosemary
1–2 tbsp, or to taste, soft brown sugar
2 tsp dry mustard powder
2 tbsp Worcestershire sauce
145 ml/5 fl oz/⅔ cup water

1   Melt the butter in a saucepan and
     gently fry the onion for 4 minutes,
     stirring frequently.

2   Add the tomato purée and continue
     to fry for 2 minutes. Blend the
     remaining ingredients together
     then add to the pan, bring to a boil.
     Reduce the heat and simmer for
     8–10 minutes or until a thick sauce
     consistency is reached. Use
     as required.

Mint Sauce

Makes 85 ml/3 fl oz/1/2 cup

25 g/1 oz/2 tbsp fresh mint sprigs
2 tsp superfine sugar or clear honey
2 tbsp boiling water
2 tbsp white wine vinegar
1 tbsp balsamic vinegar

Mint sauce is a classic and super simple.
Ideal to serve with all lamb dishes. Try
adding a spoonful or two to a lamb
casserole or stew.

1   Strip off the mint leaves from the stalks and chop finely. Place in a small bowl and add the sugar
    or honey.

2   Pour over the boiling water, stir well then leave for 5 minutes. Add both vinegars, stir well and pour into
    a sauce boat. Leave for 1 hour before using.

Salmon Ceviche

Serves 4
350 g/12 oz fresh salmon filet, skinned
145 ml/5 fl oz/⅔ cup lime juice
2 tbsp sherry vinegar
1 tbsp balsamic vinegar
1 bag salad leaves
100 g/4 oz/¾ cup cherry tomatoes, halved
small piece cucumber, sliced

Although this is not strictly a preserve in the conventional sense, the vinegar in the recipe preserves
the salmon rather than cooking it. Other very fresh fish can be used in this manner – try cod, haddock,
monkfish or trout.

1   Lightly rinse the salmon and cut into small cubes; place in a bowl. Blend the lime juice with the vinegars
    and pour over the salmon. Cover and
    leave in the refrigerator to marinate
    for at least 12 hours or overnight if
    possible. Stir occasionally.

2   When ready to serve, arrange
    the salad leaves on
    4 individual plates
    and arrange the
    tomatoes and
    cucumber on top.
    Drain the salmon
    and place on
    top of the salad
    and serve.

Mango, Apricot & Cranberry Chutney

Makes about 1.5 kg/3 lb
8 ripe but still firm mangos
450 g/1 lb/c. 5 fresh apricots
225 g/8 oz fresh cranberries
450 g/1 lb/3 cups onions, peeled and chopped
2–4 green chilies, seeded and chopped
3 garlic cloves, peeled and chopped
7.5 cm/3 in-piece fresh ginger, grated
460 ml/¾ pt/2 cups cider vinegar
550 g/1 lb 4 oz/2½ cups soft light brown sugar
½ tsp salt
juice from 1 large lemon (about 4 tbsp)

You can vary the flavor of this chutney
by using different fruits and vinegar.
Simply use this as your basic recipe.

1   Peel the mangos, discard the stones and roughly chop the flesh. Place in a non-reactive preserving
    or large pan. Stone the apricots, chop roughly and add to the pan together with all the remaining
    ingredients.

2   Place over a gentle heat and heat until the sugar has completely dissolved, stirring occasionally.

3   Bring to a boil, reduce the heat to a simmer and cook for 1 hour or until really soft and a thick
    consistency is reached. Taste and adjust sweetness then pot in clean sterilized jars. When cold, cover,
    label and store in a cool dark place for 1 month before using.

Mixed Pickles

Makes 900 g/2 lb/4 cups
900 g/2 lbs/4 cups mixed vegetables such as cauliflower, broccoli, shallots, cucumber, French/green beans, zucchini and carrots
3 tbsp salt
1 litre/2 pints/4½ cups spiced vinegar (see page 243)

All manner of vegetables can be used for this pickle. It is ideal for pickling excess vegetables when they are in
season and there is a glut.

1   If using cauliflower or broccoli, break into small florets, peel the shallots and cucumber and discard the seeds. Trim the beans and wash thoroughly, then chop into small pieces. Peel the zucchini if using and cut into small chunks. Peel the carrots and dice.

2   Dissolve the salt in 1 litre/2 pints/4½ cups water. Place all the vegetables in a large bowl and pour over the brine. Leave overnight.

3   Next day, rinse thoroughly, rinsing at least 3–4 times to remove any excess salt, then drain and dry on clean cloths. Pack into sterilized jars and cover with the vinegar. Cover with non reactive lids. label and store in a cool dark place.

Fluffy Meringue

Makes one 18-cm/7-inch case
2 medium egg whites
100 g/4 oz/½ cup superfine sugar
1 tsp raspberry vinegar
1 tsp vanilla extract

Although only a little vinegar is used here, it is surprising what a
difference it makes.

1   Preheat the oven to 150°C/fan oven 130°C/300°F/Gas Mark 2 and line a baking sheet with non-stick
    baking paper. Mark an 18-cm/7-inch circle on the paper.

2   Whisk the egg whites until stiff then gradually whisk in the sugar a spoonful at a time. When all the
    sugar has been added stir in the vinegar with the vanilla extract.

3   Place the meringue in the center of the drawn circle and shape into a large case. Bake in the preheated
    oven for 1½ hours or until set and firm to the touch. Remove from the oven, leave until cold before
    using or storing in an airtight tin.

Balsamic Flavored Strawberries

Give your guests a surprise by not telling them what you have sprinkled over the fruit and see how many guess.

1   Hull and lightly rinse some large strawberries and cut in half or quarters. Place in a glass bowl. Pour over 2–3 tablespoons balsamic vinegar. Allow to stand for 1–5 minutes.

2   Sprinkle with 1–2 tablespoons superfine sugar. Stir and serve with ice cream or cream.

Index

Recipes have uppercase initials.

A
air fresheners 60, 110
  light bulb freshener 111
air humidifiers 113
aluminum pans 39
anemia 187
animal repellents 126–7
ankles, swollen 177
anti-inflammatory 191
ants 123
anxiety 192–93
appetite 202
apple cider vinegar 168
  be prepared 170–71
  drawbacks 170
  multipurpose natural
    remedy 169–70
  reliable remedy? 170
  soft skin 147
arthritis 191–92
asthma 195
athlete's foot 178
attics 43
awnings 104

B
baby care 208–10
  cleaning and odor
    removal 211–14
baby clothes 78–79, 214
baby's bottle 213
  teats and pacifiers 213
bad breath 197

baking soda 6–8
  alternative names 8
  not to be confused with 8
Balsamic Flavored
  Strawberries 251
ballpoint stains 77
basements 43
bathrooms 46, 64–71
  all-over clean 64
  bathroom trash cans 71
  sweet smells 65
baths 66
  baby bath 209
  baking soda bath oil 147
  baking soda bath salts 146
  nonslip strips 66
BBQ Sauce 246
beauty tips 142
  body odor 164–65
  hair and nails 155–60
  skin 143–54
    teeth and mouth 161–63
berry stains 53
bicarbonate of soda 8
birdbaths 104
blackheads 151
blankets 41
  blanket reviver 91
blinds 36
blood pressure, high 187–88
bloodstains 73–74
body massage 147–48
body odor 164–65
bolts 100
books 44
brass pans 39
bread boxes 63
brickwork 101

broiler pans 52
bronchitis 196
bruises 154, 182
burns 101, 143, 183

C
cage cleaning 133
  bird cages 133–34
calluses 178–79
can openers 52
candle wax, removing
  22–23
carpets 30–31, 112
  getting sick off 31–32
  odor removal 40
  preventative strike 31
cats
  cat deterrents 126–27
  housebreaking 127, 137
  presents 130
  presents of dead mice 45
  scratching posts (not) 138
cellars 43
cellulite 181
cement burns 101
cement painting 100
chickenpox spots 184
chilblains 177
china 51
cholesterol, high 188
chrome 38, 109
Chutney, Mango, Apricot &
  Cranberry 248
Classic Vinaigrette 244
cleaning around the house
  20–23
  bathrooms 64–71

floors and walls 29–31
furnishings and surfaces
  24–28
kitchens 46–61
metal cleaning 36–39
odor removal 40–45
windows 34–36
closets 45
cockroaches 124
cold sores 174
colds 188–90
combs 156
concrete burns 101
congestion 188–89
  tight chests 190
constipation 200
contact lenses 173
cooking smells 45
cool boxes 62
copper pans 39
cork flooring 29
corns 178–79
coughs 190
cradle cap treatment
  209–10
cramps 201
crayon marks 32, 213
creases 92
  crease-free clothes 91
Crème Fraîche Dressing 245
cribs 211
culinary tips 231–34
cups 51
cuticle softener 160
cutting boards 28, 50
cuts 185

D
dandruff 158
de-icer 109
decking 104
decorations 114
degreasers 23, 25, 55
dentures 163
deodorant stains 82–83
depression 193
detox diets 202–203
diapers 78, 214
  diaper bucket 214
  diaper rash treatment
    209–10
diarrhea 200
digestion aid 198
dishcloths 48
dishwashers 48–49, 59
dishwashing 47–52
disinfectant 22
dogs
  anti-barking training
    136–37
  anti-biting training
    (puppies) 137
  coat conditioning
    spray 135
  dog presents 130
  drinking water 138
  housebreaking 137
  washing 129
door furniture 38
drains 20, 55, 67, 111
dressings
  Classic Vinaigrette 244
  Crème Fraîche
    Dressing 245
  Lemon Salad Dressing 239
'dry cleaning' 88
  shiny seats on skirts and
    trousers 92
dust 99

E
earache 175
eczema 180

electrical fires 108
eyes, itchy 173
  sore and puffy 173

F
fabric conditioner 90–1
fabric dressings 78
fainting 193–94
fatigue 193–94
fever reduction 191
fibroids 202
fingerprints 98
fingertip splits 176
fire extinguishing 108
fireplace odors 112–13
fish tanks 134
fleas 123
floors 29–31
  hard flooring cleaner 30
flowers 121–22
Fluffy Meringue 250
fly traps 125–26
foot care 166
  soothe sore, aching feet
    167
footwear 42
  salt marks 89
  whitening athletic shoes 86
Formica 54
freezers 59
fridges 58, 60
fruit and fruit juice stains
  86–87
furniture 24–26
  garden furniture 103
  ring stains on furniture
    24–25
  white painted furniture 24
furniture polish 27
furniture wax and polish
  build-up 27

G
gall stones 204–205
garden furniture 103
  repairs 106

garden pots 102
garden tools 102
gardening uses 116–21
garlic smells 61
glass cleaning 34–35
  bug removal 109
glasses 51
gold 38
gout 192
grazes 185
grease stains 76
greenhouse fungicide 118
greenhouse wash 117
grill cleaning 103
grout 33, 71
gum disease 174

H
hair 155–59
  conditioner 155–56
  hair loss 158
  natural hairspray 159
  shampoo 155
  shiny hair 157
  sun-kissed hair 157
  treating damaged or
    colored hair 157–58
hairbrushes 156
hammocks 105
hand-washing 80
hands 62, 165–66
  dry hands 176
  moisturizer 145
hangovers 197
hay fever 196
head lice 175–76
headaches 197–98
heart palpitations 206
hemorrhoids 200
hiccups 196
holiday decorations 114
Hollandaise Sauce 244–45
Hot Lemon Punch 240
houseflies 125
household uses 96
  holiday lemons 114

lemon freshness 110–13
  maintenance and DIY
    97–101
  outdoors 102–109

I
ice 106
immune system
  strengthening 191
indigestion 198–99
ink stains 30, 77, 144–45
insect bites and stings 138,
  184–5
insect-free paintwork 126
insecticides 125
insomnia 194
intestines 204
iron sole plate cleaning 81
ivory surfaces 27–28

J
jewelry 37–38
joint pain 192

K
kettle de-scaler 59
kidney stones 205–206
kit bags 43
kitchens 46–61
  kitchen appliances 56–59
  kitchen trash cans 63
  kitchen cabinets 54
  kitchen sinks 47, 54–55
  kitchen surfaces 53–55
  kitchen utensils 51
  odor removal 60–63
kitty litter 132

L
laminates 26
laundry 72, 78–80
  collars and cuffs 76
  coloreds 85–86, 92
  conditioning 90–93
  killing bacteria 89
  reshaping woolens 92

stain and odor removal
73–77, 81–83, 86–88
stop red running 92
vintage lace restored 88
whites 83–85
laundry baskets 83
homemade sachets 83
lavatories 66
cisterns 67
toilet seats 67
lawns 119
leather 77
leather furniture 25–26
lemons 12, 218
beauty benefits 14
buying 15
candied lemon peel 222
decorations 114
glass cleaning 35
household uses 14
juicing 16–17
lemon extract and
powder 222
lemon freshness 110–13
lemon metal cleaner 39
lemon oil 110
lemon pepper 220
lemon sugar 222
lemon trees 12–13
lemon zest 17, 220
lemony smell 14–15
nutrients 13–14
preparing 16
preserved lemons 223
storing 16
versatility 13
waxed or unwaxed? 15
lemon recipes
Hot Lemon Punch 240
Lemon Barley Water 236
Lemon Curd 238
Lemon Salad Dressing 239
Lemon Sorbet 237–38
Lemonade 235

limescale build-up 22, 65,
68–69
lino 29
lint removal 91
lips, chapped 173
liver 204
lockers 43
lofts 43
luggage 43

M
Mango, Apricot & Cranberry
Chutney 248
marble surfaces 27–28
mattresses 41
mealy bugs 127
meat preparation 224–25
Meringue, Fluffy 250
metabolic rate increase
203–204
metal cleaner 36, 39
metal furniture 26
metal painting 100
metalware 38
microwaves 57–58
mildew 99
mildew on clothes 81
mildew on garden furniture
and decks 104
mildew on luggage 43
mineral build-up 22
Mint Sauce 246–47
mirrors 35
wing mirrors 109
Mixed Pickles 248–49
mold 63
moldy shower curtains
69–70
mothballs 111
moths 126
mouth 161–63, 173–74, 197
cleaning on the move
162–63
mouth ulcers 198
mugs 51
muscles, sore 186

N
nails 159–60
nail polish 160
shiny nails 159
strong nails 160
natural remedies 172
hands and feet 176–79
head and face 173–76
internal health 187–207
skin and body 179–86
nausea 199
nerve pain 192
nose bleeds 175

O
odor removal 40–45
banish smells from suits 88
bathrooms 71
cars 107–108
cutting boards 28, 50
dishwashers 48–49
drains 111
fireplaces 112–13
kitchens 60–63
microwaves 58
mothballs 111
paint fumes 99
pet bedding 130–31
second-hand clothing 88
oil stains 107
onion smells 61
ovens 56–57
oven doors 57
oven spritzer 57

P
paint fumes 99
paintbrush restoration 98–99
patios 104
patio umbrellas 104
paving 104
pearlash 7
perspiration stains 75, 82
pest control 116–27
petrol stains 107
pets 128

bedding 130–31
bites and stings 138
bowls 134
cleaning 129–34
collars and leashes 132
ear cleaning 135–36
health 135–38
toys 132
Pickles, Mixed 248–49
picnic hampers 62
pimples 151
plant diseases 118–19
cleaning spray bottles 118
plastering 97
plastic containers 52, 61
playpens 211
plugholes 20, 55, 111
poison ivy 180
pomanders 114
pools, inflatable 103
pot pourri 113
pots and pans 39, 49
burned-on food 49
non-stick pans 47, 50
soaking 49
poultry preparation 224–25
psoriasis 179–80

R
rabbits 124
rashes 79
razor burn 143
retainers 163
rose spray 118
Rose Vinegar 242–43
Rosemary Vinegar 241–42
rubber gloves 48
rugs 112
rust stains 75–76
rusty bikes 109
rusty garden tools 102
rusty metal 26, 100

S
salad crispers 60
Salmon Ceviche 247